DATE DUE

D1551151

The American Association of Community Colleges (AACC)
is the primary advocacy organization for the nation's community colleges. The association represents 1,100 two-year,
associate degree-granting institutions and some 10 million
students. AACC provides leadership and service in five key
areas: policy initiatives, advocacy, research, education services,
and coordination/networking.

© 2001 American Association of Community Colleges

All rights reserved. No part of this book may be reproduced
or transmitted in any form or by any means, electronic
or mechanical, including, without limitation, photocopying,
recording, or by any information storage and retrieval system,
without written permission.

Requests for permission should be sent to
Community College Press
American Association of Community Colleges
One Dupont Circle, NW
Suite 410
Washington, DC 20036
Fax: (202) 223-9390

Printed in the United States of America.

ISBN 0-87117-332-8

Right: The South Doors, Joliet Junior College, Illinois

AMERICA'S COMMUNITY COLLEGES

A Century of Innovation

COMMUNITY COLLEGE PRESS®

a division of the American Association of Community Colleges

Washington, D.C.

CONTENTS

The work celebrates the potential for achievement within each student and each college, at this centennial and every day.

The American Association of Community Colleges (AACC) celebrates the centennial of community colleges with this pictorial tribute, *America's Community Colleges: A Century of Innovation.* ■ The book features distinguished community college alumni and is organized according to major career fields for which community colleges commonly prepare students. Some categories will overlap, as the fields are broadly generalized. The photographs were graciously submitted by community colleges in response to an open invitation and were selected based on print quality and variety. The text was drawn from interviews and information submitted for the AACC Outstanding Alumni Awards. ■ Although many forces contributed to the inception of the community college, AACC recognizes 100 years starting in 1901 with the opening of Joliet Junior College in Illinois, the oldest continuously operating public two-year college. The list of colleges appearing in the book's margin consists of independently regionally accredited two-year institutions; it includes districts and university two-year branch campuses but does not include names of individual campuses unless they are independently accredited. The list also includes community colleges in outlying territories such as Palau and Guam. ■ Unfortunately, it was not possible to include a text reference or photo for every college, program, idea, student, or highly dedicated person who has contributed to student success. Omissions are inevitable and sincerely regretted. Yet, the publication offers a sense of the rich contributions made by community colleges and their students to our nation—a glimpse of the community college impact. ■ Although it is natural to appreciate the accomplishments of distinguished and famous alumni, the book's overriding purpose is to recognize the commitment made by community colleges to more than 10 million students per year through credit and noncredit courses; the capacity of institutions to effect positive change through ingenuity and collaboration; and the ability of people to improve, enhance, and even transform their lives through education. The work celebrates the potential for achievement within each student and each college, at this centennial and every day.

History in the Making

"WHATEVER FORM THE COMMUNITY COLLEGE TAKES, ITS PURPOSE IS EDUCATIONAL
SERVICE TO THE ENTIRE COMMUNITY, AND THIS PURPOSE REQUIRES OF IT
A VARIETY OF FUNCTIONS AND PROGRAMS."

— *Higher Education for American Democracy (Truman Commission report, 1947)*

Great challenges faced the United States in the early 20th century, including global economic competition. National and local leaders realized that a more skilled workforce was key to the country's continued economic strength—a need that called for a dramatic increase in college attendance—yet three-quarters of high school graduates were choosing not to further their education, in part because they were reluctant to leave home for a distant college.

During the same period, the country's rapidly growing public high schools were seeking new ways to serve their communities. It was common for them to add a teacher institute, manual learning (vocational education) division, or citizenship school to the diploma program. The high school-based community college, as first developed at Central High School in Joliet, Illinois *(left, under renovation in 1924)*, was the most successful type of addition. Meanwhile, small, private colleges

Looking solemn for the camera, the 1914 graduating class of St. Philip's College in Texas prepares to go out into the world. St. Philip's was founded as a parochial day school with just one class, sewing instruction, for 20 African American girls. Under the leadership of Artemisia Bowden, the daughter of a former Georgia slave, St. Philip's grew to become an industrial school and a fully accredited public junior college in 1942.

The Rogers-Carrier House (below) is one of several historic homes on Michigan's Lansing Community College campus. LCC serves 40,000 students annually. Among future students will be some who have their course charted from birth: The college awards a two-semester scholarship each year to the first baby born in April (national community college month) to residents of the LCC district.

"Gateway to Success" reads the inscription above the Gould Memorial Library at New York's Bronx Community College, a branch campus of the City University of New York. The turn-of-the-century building, designed by renowned architect Stanford White, was part of the University Heights campus of New York University until 1973, when BCC took over the site.

With the help of an instructor, a soldier recently returned from World War II learns the touch-typing method at California's College of San Mateo. The passage of the GI Bill in 1944, which provided what amounted to a scholarship for all eligible veterans, broke down financial and social barriers to college for millions of Americans. It also provided a large boost in enrollments for community colleges.

such as Indiana's Vincennes University had fashioned an effective model of higher education grounded on the principles of small classes, close student-faculty relations, and a program that included both academics and extracurricular activities.

From the combination of these traditions emerged the earliest community colleges, roughly balanced in number between private and public control but united in their commitment to meet local needs. The typical early community college was small, rarely enrolling more than 150 students. It nevertheless offered a program of solid academics as well as a variety of student activities. Fort Scott Junior College in Kansas, for example, not only fielded several athletic teams but also

supported a student newspaper, government, thespian society, and orchestra.

A distinctive feature of the institutions was their accessibility to women, attributable to the leading role the colleges played in preparing grammar school teachers. In such states as Missouri, which did not yet require

Students and community college supporters helped beautify the future site of Illinois's Freeport Community College by planting trees and shrubs. These plants were the foundation of a regional arboretum now part of the college's 140-acre campus, surrounded by natural prairie, woodland, and an athletic field. Established in 1962, the institution was renamed Highland Community College in 1967.

K–8 teachers to have a bachelor's degree, it was common for more than 60 percent of community college students to be women, virtually all of them preparing to be teachers.

Between 1950 and 1980, major demographic trends brought change to community colleges, deepening their commitment to access through low cost, a comprehensive curriculum, and innovation. By 1960, states could no longer ignore the pending demand of baby boomers for access to college. Many state leaders were influenced by the 1947 Truman Commission report *Higher Education for American Democracy*, which encouraged the growth of community colleges. Some states, including Virginia and Massachusetts, created entire systems of state community colleges. Others, including California and Texas, used state resources to expand local institutions and to add new ones. During the 1960s, more than 450 new community colleges opened nationwide.

While the community colleges focused their attention on access, they still had to confront the controversy of segregation. Institutions such as St. Philip's College in Texas and Bluefield State College in West Virginia were first created to provide access to higher education for black students, but the *Brown* v. *Board of Education* case in 1954 questioned whether separate access could provide equal opportunity. Over time, community colleges eliminated or merged segregated

Berkshire Community College, the first such institution in Massachusetts, occupied the third and fourth floors of Pittsfield High School (left) when the college first opened in 1960. By 1969, the college had broken ground for a permanent campus. During the 1960s, hundreds of new community colleges opened nationwide, putting a campus within commuting distance of the majority of Americans.

Students in the sawmill trades, carpentry, electrical, and agriculture programs at North Carolina's Haywood Community College built the mill house below, a reminder of the region's Appalachian heritage. Haywood's entire campus is a designated arboretum. The mill house, a pond, and surrounding area serve as a teaching lab for students of forestry, wildlife, and horticulture.

Students line up outside the student center to register for fall classes at the new Parkland College in Illinois. Classes were held in various buildings in downtown Champaign until a permanent campus could be built. The first graduating class, in May 1968, numbered 20 students.

A line of students files into the first library on the campus of Florida's Miami-Dade Community College in the early 1960s. That decade saw many community colleges move into urban locations and become pioneers in serving diverse student populations.

Shelby State Community College was the first multicampus facility in Tennessee specifically designed to serve the diverse educational needs of a metropolitan area. The Southeast Center campus (right) opened in the Mendenhall Square Mall. In 2000, Shelby State joined with State Technical Institute at Memphis to form Southwest Tennessee Community College.

Two exuberant members of the class of 1996 celebrate graduation from California's Southwestern College. Like most community colleges, Southwestern offers disability support services such as specialized software and hardware and training with assistive technology. Community colleges serve more students with disabilities than any other sector of higher education.

When Ohio's Cuyahoga Community College opened on September 23, 1963, it experienced the largest first-day community college enrollment the nation had ever seen—more than 3,000 students. Classes were held in a 19th-century building leased from the Cleveland Board of Education. Today, Cuyahoga serves 55,000 students at three modern campuses, including the Western Campus in Parma (above), two centers, and five off-campus sites.

schools and increasingly served, valued, and actively recruited a diverse population of students.

Community colleges have held fast to their commitment to access. They have maintained affordable tuition rates, a diverse curriculum, and the developmental programs needed to provide students with the skills required for academic success. Community colleges have also reached out to new communities, to more closely align programs and services with the needs of an increasingly diverse population.

Community colleges were among the first to embrace emerging technologies to expand educational opportunity. In the 1960s, institutions such as the College of San Mateo, with its station KCSM, moved quickly to bring the classroom into the community through television. Similarly, the colleges have used adaptive technologies to enable those with disabilities to enter the educational mainstream.

Through community colleges, states not only make good on their commitment to universal access but also prepare much of the skilled workforce that has made possible the nation's continuing economic growth. Small classes and close student-faculty relations are still the norm, and the community college remains an effective career gateway for all students. In the United States, community colleges enroll nearly 50 percent of all first-time college freshmen.

With their small business centers, community colleges have become a one-stop resource for American entrepreneurs. Through short-cycle training programs, they have given dislocated workers the tools to successfully reenter the workforce. And through a campus culture that celebrates diversity, the colleges signal their readiness to serve students from all walks of life who recognize that dreams are fulfilled through education, and the door of the community college is an open door to opportunity for all.

Demonstrating that a community college is indeed a place for lifelong learning, three members of the Simkins family— parents Kathy and Mark and daughter Rebecca— graduated with the class of 1999 from New Jersey's Camden County College. Mark earned a UNIX certificate, Kathy graduated with associate degrees in business administration and information processing, and Rebecca earned an associate in arts degree and a spot on the dean's list.

1 Science & Technology

"As soon as I learned to fly, I found a whole new world that was more exciting and wonderful."

—Mildred "Micky" Tuttle Axton, first female B-29 pilot (Coffeyville Community College, Kansas)

Community colleges have long been in the forefront of preparing America's workforce for emerging technologies. With each new innovation, they have moved swiftly to create and expand programs in fields ranging from aviation and automotive science to metalworking and computer programming. At left, students at Florida's Miami-Dade Community College participate in an air traffic control laboratory, learning procedures used by the Federal Aviation Administration. Upon completion of the program, students are recommended to the FAA for employment.

Community colleges first demonstrated their commitment to providing needed training quickly during World War II, when they did their part to ready men and women for the war effort. The federal government's Civilian Pilot Training Program, introduced in 1940, was one of the new programs offered through community colleges.

One pilot who completed the training was 23-year-old Mildred "Micky" Tuttle Axton. After graduating from Coffeyville Community College in Kansas in 1938, she earned an advanced degree and then returned to

When **Micky Axton** earned her pilot's license at Coffeyville Community College in Kansas, her first passenger was her 91-year-old great-grandmother, a pioneer in the 19th century, who loved the plane ride. "She said it sure did beat covered wagons," recalls Axton, who served with the WASPs during World War II and became the first woman to pilot a B-29.

Students at California's College of San Mateo work on airplanes in the years after World War II. Aeronautics was introduced in 1932 as the college's first vocational program. Today, San Mateo offers an associate degree in science and trains students to sit for the FAA examination that leads to A&P/AMT (airframe and power-plant technician) certification.

Coffeyville as an instructor of aeronautics and chemistry. When the college began offering the pilot program, Axton immediately applied. Upon learning that she had been accepted, she was ecstatic. "The junior college was 10 blocks from our house," she recalled, "and I ran all the way there to sign the papers!" In 1943, she headed for Texas and a wartime assignment with the Women Airforce Service Pilots (WASP). She and her comrades ferried planes between bases, tested repaired planes, and towed targets for combat pilots. When she left the WASPs in 1944, Axton took a job as a flight analyst at Boeing, where she became the first woman to fly a B-29—the Superfortress.

Coffeyville and other community colleges were on the cutting edge in 1940. The same is true today, as colleges strive to meet the needs of business and industry. Miami-Dade's Eig-Watson School of Aviation offers associate in science degrees in pilot technology, aviation management, and aviation maintenance management, in addition to airline service-related certificates.

This comprehensive approach has also been adopted in other technology-related programs. Colleges have long offered generalized courses in automotive service, maintenance, and repair. Today, they train students to be dealership and independent technicians, service managers, vehicle and equipment salespeople, and machine shop operators. Some programs for service technicians are cosponsored by major automotive manufac-

A fleet of airplanes awaits students in the aviation technology program at Colorado Northwestern Community College. The program offers two options: One trains students through private, instrument, and commercial certificates in preparation for transfer to a four-year college; the other prepares pilots for immediate employment by including instrument flight-instructor and multiengine rating.

In Kansas City, Missouri, Cynthia Weeks works on an engine in one of Longview Community College's automotive technology programs. Ford Motor Company, General Motors, and Toyota cosponsor three of Longview's programs.

In 1930, a Wisconsin automotive-mechanic class poses for a picture in their shop. Vocational schools were founded in Green Bay and Marinette in 1913 to standardize the education of apprentices. Today, those two campuses and one that opened in Sturgeon Bay in 1941 compose the Northeast Wisconsin Technical College.

turers. Columbia-Greene Community College in New York requires students in its Ford ASSET (Automotive Student Specialty Educational Training) program to have a dealership sponsor.

Construction technology is another popular field. Graduates of construction programs typically take jobs as foremen, project superintendents, private contractors, draftsmen, and construction material inspectors. Many community colleges, such as Connecticut's Norwalk Community College, offer comprehensive curricula that include architectural and civil engineering courses. Others offer specialized associate degrees, such as the one in concrete technology at Michigan's Alpena Community College.

Some programs, such as those in machining, metalworking, construction, automotives, and aviation, are common among community colleges; other programs are unique. In 1988, Texarkana College in Texas found-

Michele Sohl, a concrete technology student at Michigan's Alpena Community College, places a cylinder of concrete in a compression machine to determine how many pounds per square inch of pressure the material can withstand before breaking. Graduates of the program are in high demand in a wide range of concrete-related industries, engineering and research, and construction sales and service.

Machine technology student Tom Perkins operates a milling machine at Orange Coast College in California. The device has been retrofitted to allow Perkins, who uses a wheelchair, to adjust the machine pneumatically rather than manually.

John D. Mendiola, a student in Salem Community College's scientific glass technology program, shapes a flask. The New Jersey college offers the country's only associate degree in this field and attracts enrollees from around the world.

A Texarkana College student forges a blade. To preserve this ancient craft, the college joined with the Pioneer Washington Restoration Foundation and the American Bladesmith Society to establish the Bill Moran School of Bladesmithing in Washington, Arkansas. Courses are taught in a replica of a one-room schoolhouse and in a barn, blending in with the town's old-time atmosphere.

ed the Bill Moran School of Bladesmithing, which instructs students in the art of forging knife blades. Fittingly, the program is located in nearby Washington, Arkansas, a restoration of the 19th-century town where the first bowie knife was reputedly forged.

No less specialized is the scientific glass blowing program offered by New Jersey's Salem Community College, in which students learn to cut, heat, bend, shape, and seal glass and to understand blueprint reading and advanced fabrication. Most graduates find employment in industry, research, or manufacturing. Others, like Paul Stankard of Mantua, New Jersey, become a cottage industry unto themselves. Stankard initially found work developing specialized glassware at a petrochemical plant. In his free time, he crafted realistic glass paperweights drawn from botanical images. Today, his artwork is featured in galleries in New York and is the basis of a family business.

Students who pursue careers in science may select from a wide variety of programs. Community college offerings run the gamut from traditional biology, chemistry, and botany to more specialized fields, in-

Amid a shower of sparks, a safety-garbed welder (right) practices his technique at Spokane Community College in Washington. The demand for trained welders rose during the 1990s, in part because of the retirement of many older workers and the aging of the nation's infrastructure.

*Undersea explorer **Sylvia A. Earle** pauses on a dive ladder. A graduate of St. Petersburg Junior College in Florida, Earle has participated in more than 50 expeditions and founded a company to design robotics for undersea exploration. As National Geographic's Explorer in Residence, she monitors underwater sanctuaries and directs research projects such as the Sustainable Seas Expeditions.*

Michael Hutchins, *director of conservation and science at the American Zoo and Aquarium Association, poses with a koala. Hutchins, who embarked on his college education at Highline Community College in Washington, fights to protect endangered species. "If we lose nature," he told the Louisville Courier-Journal, "something in our souls will be gone."*

NATURAL SCIENCES

Reathel Geary, *one-time student at North Carolina's Asheville-Buncombe Technical Community College, examines a plant in his botany laboratory at North Carolina State University. In a national competition, officials selected Geary's research project on plant DNA for inclusion on a 1998 space shuttle flight.*

cluding marine science, wastewater treatment, and air-quality management.

Few people have made a more lasting mark in marine science than Sylvia Earle, a 1953 graduate of Florida's St. Petersburg Junior College and a renowned scientist and explorer. In 1970, Earle, who earned a Ph.D. from Duke University, was chosen to lead an all-female research expedition, Tektite II, Mission 6, jointly sponsored by the U.S. Navy, the Department of the Interior, and NASA. Earle and her four aquanaut companions spent two weeks in an enclosed habitat 50 feet below the surface of the sea.

"I really slept as little as I could get by with so that I could be out there with the fish," Earle later recalled. "I'd get up before dawn so that I could watch the changeover time, when the ones that are active at night tuck in and the day fish come out."

Tektite was only one of Earle's voyages to the bottom of the sea. In 1979, she walked on the ocean floor at the incredible depth of 1,250 feet. Attached to a submarine by only a communication line, Earle explored "bioluminescent creatures flashing with their blue fire" and a fantastic, six-foot-high field of coral: "If I touched up near the top, you could see the pulses of blue, like little blue donuts of light." In the past two decades, Earle has further advanced marine science by founding two companies, Deep Ocean Exploration and Research, which develops and builds small submarines for exploration, and DOER Marine Operations, which provides consulting and marine engineering services.

The 1980s and 1990s saw tremendous strides in a range of science and technology fields, as advances in one field stimulated others. In 1984, Pasadena City College, California, alumnus Bruce Merrifield received the Nobel Prize in chemistry for work he began in the 1950s and 1960s originating solid-phase peptide synthesis, a process of synthesizing proteins that improved the safety and effectiveness of a variety of medications. He has received numerous other awards for his work in chemistry.

On the frontier of genetic science, J. Craig Venter is a leading figure in the race to decode the human genome—all the genetic material within a human cell. Venter started his higher education in 1969 at the College of San Mateo in California, following a three-year stint as a medical corpsman during the Vietnam War. From San Mateo, Venter transferred to the University of California, San Diego, where he received a bachelor's degree in biochemistry and a doctorate in physiology and pharmacology. Some years later, he founded The Institute for Genomic Research (TIGR), a not-for-profit research institution. There Venter developed a technique that drastically shortened the time necessary for

Student Eric Neel (above) examines a turtle in Costa Rica's Tortuguero National Park. Neel's environmental biology class from Tomball College, Texas, traveled to Costa Rica to study the area's diversity of animal species and gain a greater understanding of endangered tropical ecosystems.

Elizabeth Cowan and Sam Goodwin learn about industrial water treatment in a San Juan College laboratory in Farmington, New Mexico. They are studying a reverse-osmosis system that eliminates impurities from drinking water.

Sherry Heldens (right), a research assistant in the DNA sequencing lab at Genentech's Department of Molecular Biology, credits the City College of San Francisco with her professional success. "The education and experience I gained at CCSF allow me to work alongside people with bachelor's and master's degrees, doing comparable work for comparable pay."

Below, students at California's Santa Monica College work in a laboratory in the college's science complex. Replacing a building destroyed in an earthquake, the complex, which opened in 1999, houses state-of-the-art laboratories, multimedia classrooms, and student learning centers.

In Dayton, Ohio, in the 1920s, an all-male class studies chemistry at the YMCA College, which became Sinclair College in 1948. Sinclair traces its roots to 1887, when the local YMCA began offering evening classes. It gradually expanded its courses and eventually offered college-level instruction.

identifying the tens of thousands of genes in the coiled strands of DNA that make up human chromosomes.

In 1999, Venter astounded the scientific community by announcing that his new corporation, Celera Genomics, in collaboration with the Berkeley Drosophila Genome Project, had decoded the complete genome for the fruit fly. This amazing feat—the first mapping of the genome for a higher-level organism—proved that Venter's technique worked. In June 2000, Celera announced the first assembly of the human genome.

Growing enrollments in computer science and technology programs indicate that community colleges have become the provider of choice for students seeking computer training. Many students gain their first access to a computer when they enroll at a

community college, and the colleges are helping to narrow the "digital divide" between people who have computer skills and those who do not. As information technology (IT) careers expand, community college programs have increased accordingly, often in response to the needs of local and national businesses.

In an example of the growing collaboration between industry and community colleges, Microsoft and the American Association of Community Colleges established a joint initiative, Working Connections, to help the colleges develop and enhance IT training. One Working Connections mentor college, De Anza College in California, enrolls more than 7,000 students in its computer information systems department. Danny Nguyen, a successful program graduate, "felt like a nobody going nowhere" before he enrolled at De Anza.

J. Craig Venter, an alumnus of California's College of San Mateo, developed a revolutionary strategy for gene sequencing. Having reached this milestone, which could eventually transform the understanding, treatment, and prevention of disease, Venter aims to sequence the proteins that drive the body's chemical reactions.

CONNECTICUT

ASNUNTUCK COMMUNITY COLLEGE

BRIARWOOD COLLEGE

CAPITAL COMMUNITY COLLEGE—WOODLAND

GATEWAY COMMUNITY COLLEGE

HOUSATONIC COMMUNITY COLLEGE

INTERNATIONAL COLLEGE OF HOSPITALITY MANAGEMENT— CESAR RITZ

MANCHESTER COMMUNITY COLLEGE

MIDDLESEX COMMUNITY COLLEGE

MITCHELL COLLEGE

NAUGATUCK VALLEY COMMUNITY COLLEGE

NORTHWESTERN CONNECTICUT COMMUNITY COLLEGE

NORWALK COMMUNITY COLLEGE

QUINEBAUG VALLEY COMMUNITY COLLEGE

ST. VINCENT'S COLLEGE

THREE RIVERS COMMUNITY COLLEGE

TUNXIS COMMUNITY TECHNICAL COLLEGE

DELAWARE

DELAWARE TECHNICAL AND COMMUNITY COLLEGE

FLORIDA

BREVARD COMMUNITY COLLEGE

BROWARD COMMUNITY COLLEGE

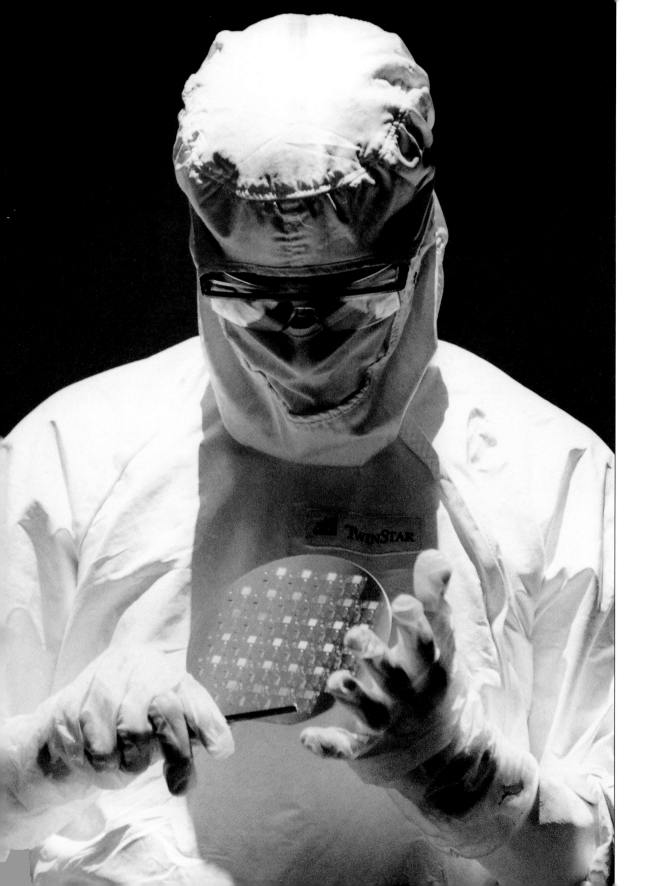

Three months after completing his training, Nguyen was employed by a leading IT firm. Working Connections, he said, "changed the entire course of my life."

Another company that takes an interest in community colleges is Cisco Systems, which develops hardware and software for linking computer networks. In spring 2000, Cisco selected six community colleges to serve as regional training centers for Cisco instructors. According to Peter Brierley, technology professor and coordinator of the Cisco academy program at Collin County Community College in Texas, Cisco-certified graduates are in very high demand.

The demand for systems designers, Web page designers, network specialists, and electronic commerce experts has spurred a number of community colleges to offer certificate and associate degree programs in Internet technologies. Chuck Chulvic, dean of academic services at Raritan Valley Community College, New Jersey, says, "We wanted a certification program that would enable students to go beyond the technical and allow them to become well rounded—able to design new media, do project management, and have other attributes that go beyond technical school."

Like industry, federal agencies are working with community colleges to strengthen students' knowledge of the sciences. During the summer of 1999, students from community colleges across the nation participated in the U.S. Department of Energy's eight-week In-

Wearing a suit that will protect him and the device he is working on from contaminants, student Mike Savboda (left) learns to manufacture semiconductors at Collin County Community College in Texas. In the late 1990s, Collin County partnered with Dallas County Community College District's Richland College and semiconductor companies to create a program that trains students to work with the latest equipment and technology in the field.

stitute of Biotechnology, Environmental Science, and Computing for Community Colleges, held at several of the department's national laboratories. The institute afforded students an extraordinary opportunity to work with world-class scientists. Student Brian Budzynski of Waubonsee Community College in Illinois spoke enthusiastically about his "exposure to so many new and different topics in science and engineering."

When Joseph C. Simmons graduated from Utah's Dixie College in 1955, he could not have known how far his community college experience would take him. After completing an engineering degree at the University of Utah, he took a job with McDonnell Douglas (now the Boeing Company), where he was one of the team that developed the Thor booster rocket. Shortly after the Soviet Union launched the Sputnik satellite, Simmons was charged with matching that

Miami-Dade Community College in Florida has offered computer courses for nearly four decades, as evidenced by this photo of a 1965 computer lab. Like other community colleges, Miami-Dade makes computer training a priority, keeping at the fore of its mission "the importance of technology in the up-to-date, cutting-edge educational preparation of our students."

Eileen Collins, a graduate of New York's Corning Community College, was a pilot instructor and a professor of mathematics at the U.S. Air Force Academy in Colorado before becoming a NASA astronaut in 1991. On her first voyage in space, in 1995, Collins became the first female pilot of a U.S. space shuttle. In 1999, on her third flight, she became the first woman to command a shuttle mission.

Robert L. "Hoot" Gibson, a 1966 graduate of Suffolk County Community College in New York, took the college banner with him on his 1989 flight aboard the space shuttle Atlantis. As a NASA astronaut, Gibson completed five space missions and returned to Suffolk County to talk with students about his experiences.

Fred W. Haise, a graduate of Perkinston Junior College (now Mississippi Gulf Coast Community College) in Mississippi, became an astronaut in 1966 and was the lunar module pilot for the extraordinary Apollo 13 mission four years later. Haise retired in 1996 as president of Northrup Grumman Technical Services.

ASTRONAUTS

An alumnus of Florida's St. Petersburg Junior College and a doctor of astrogeophysics, **Samuel T. Durrance** flew as a payload specialist for NASA in the early 1990s. He became a principal research scientist in Johns Hopkins University's physics and astronomy department.

Richard Welch crouches beside a planetary exploration device called a rover (left). Welch, a graduate of Berkshire Community College in Massachusetts, develops robotics for the Jet Propulsion Laboratory at the California Institute of Technology. He worked on the rover Sojourner, part of the 1997 Pathfinder mission to Mars. He and other engineers sent daily commands to the rover.

accomplishment. In 1958, he and his teammates used the Thor booster to put the first U.S. satellite—a 35-pound radio transmitter—into space. Over an impressive 40-year career, Simmons rose to the head of Product Engineering and Definition in McDonnell Douglas's Space Transportation division.

The space industry has attracted many community college graduates. Engineer Tony Springer, a graduate of Kankakee Community College in Illinois, began his relationship with NASA in 1989 as a cooperative education student, while he was still at Kankakee. After completing a bachelor's degree in aeronautical and astronautical engineering at the University of Illinois, he went to work for the agency full time. In August 1999, Springer received the Marshall Space Flight Center Research and Technology Award for notable achievement in current technology development. Springer has been involved with NASA's design of the x-34, a reusable space vehicle.

Community college alumni are also found among NASA's most illustrious team members: the astronauts. In 1995, Eileen M. Collins—who received an associate in science degree in 1976 from New York's Corning Community College—piloted the space shuttle during the first flight of the joint Russian-American Space Program. Robert L. "Hoot" Gibson, a graduate of New York's Suffolk County Community College, became an astronaut in 1979 and completed five space missions before retiring to become a commercial pilot. Gibson once arranged a "hookup"—voice communication—with Suffolk County students while he was in orbit on the space shuttle. Samuel T. Durrance, a 1967 graduate of St. Petersburg Junior College, Florida, not only flew as a payload specialist on the shuttles *Columbia* and *Endeavour* in the early 1990s but also has developed space hardware, including telescopes, spectrometers, and imaging systems. James A. McDivitt, an alumnus of

Jackson Community College in Michigan, was the command pilot for *Gemini 4* and commander of the *Apollo 9* mission in the 1960s.

One of the most memorable of all NASA missions belongs to Fred W. Haise, a 1952 graduate of Perkinston Junior College, now Mississippi Gulf Coast Community College. Haise was a crew member aboard the ill-fated *Apollo 13*. Against enormous odds, he and fellow astronauts James A. Lovell and John L. Swigert coaxed their damaged craft safely to earth with the assistance of engineers and scientists at the mission control center in Houston.

Meeting the challenges of a century, community colleges and their alumni have contributed determination, resourcefulness, and ingenuity to the world of science and technology.

The 83-foot Mercury Redstone rocket stands sentinel before the golden geodesic dome of the Michigan Space and Science Center on the campus of Jackson Community College. The center houses some $30 million worth of space artifacts and displays. The center's location is a tribute to the many astronauts who are associated with Michigan, including James McDivitt, command pilot for Gemini 4 and commander of the Apollo 9 mission.

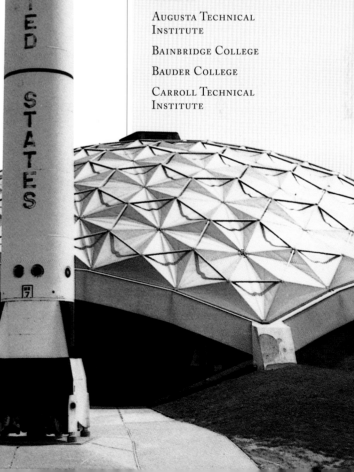

Designs That Reflect Life

"COMFORT. EASE. LUXURY. LONGEVITY. THAT'S MY FASHION PHILOSOPHY, AND I REPEAT IT EVERY TIME I DESIGN A NEW COLLECTION."

—Karen Kane, fashion designer (Fashion Institute of Design and Merchandising, California)

Popular wisdom has it that fashion reflects life, and each year thousands of community college students and graduates share their interpretations of the times with the buying public. Some of these eager and talented new designers emerge from institutions that are dedicated solely to teaching the design, manufacture, and marketing of apparel, accessories, jewelry, home furnishings, and other related products. Others complete their course work at colleges where this field of study is just one of the many offered. But all design graduates have one goal in common: to develop a successful career based on their unique personal vision.

Colleges devoted to particular fields tend to have close relationships with their related industries, and community colleges featuring fashion design are no exception. In Los Angeles, for example, the Fashion Institute of Design and Merchandising (FIDM) works closely with the Academy of Motion Picture Arts and Sciences. Each year, Academy Award nominees for best costume are displayed at FIDM's gallery and museum, where academy board members evaluate them before the Oscar ceremonies. The Texas Food and Fibers Commission sponsors a natural-fiber fashion design competition each spring. Design students from com-

As her tape measure-wielding students look on, a Fashion Institute of Technology, New York, instructor goes over the finer points of measuring a customer for a girdle during a foundations class in 1950. Fashion design students put such fundamentals as ensuring a perfect fit into practice with their own creations, including the elegant evening gown at left, designed by an FIT student.

*FIT graduate **Vy Higginsen** drew on her background in fashion, advertising, publishing, and theater to write, produce, and direct Mama, I Want to Sing, the longest-running off-Broadway black musical in the history of American theater.*

*Designer **Karen Kane**, a 1976 graduate of the Fashion Institute of Design and Merchandising in Los Angeles, began her career as a patternmaker. Karen Kane, Inc., the women's clothing company she and her husband launched from their garage in 1979, now enjoys annual sales of $75 million.*

*An alumna of Miss Wade's Fashion Merchandising College (now Wade College) in Dallas and founder of Christi Harris Companies, Inc., an international cosmetics firm, **Christi Harris Speer** teaches skin-care theory and educates consumers about beauty products.*

*After 12 years of designing sportswear for retailers, FIT graduate **Mary Ann Restivo**, designer and president of Mary Ann Restivo, Inc., has opened the doors of her New York showroom to consumers, selling a line of clothing directly to clients.*

FASHION DESIGNERS

***David Chu** briefly considered architecture before discovering his true calling in a summer drawing class at FIT. In 1983, with six men's outerwear designs in hand, he founded Nautica International, Inc., now a billion-dollar apparel company.*

*FIT student **Dave Allen Tillett** won an international design competition in 1997 with his line of all-American, surfing-inspired beach- and evening-wear for women. This red, white, and blue swimsuit (background) comes with a life vest and flotation device.*

Fashion marketing students at Waukesha County Technical College in Wisconsin model apparel they created for a Make-It-Yourself with Wool national competition in the 1970s. Fashion marketing is now part of WCTC's retail management program. Through an agreement with Milwaukee's Mount Mary College, program graduates may transfer directly to the four-year college.

Student models from the design program at Houston Community College show off their creations. Since 1982, the college's students have taken part in international study tours, during which they acquaint themselves with design technology in Paris, Milan, Hong Kong, and other locales.

munity colleges and universities across the state create original garments from three Texas-produced textiles—cotton, wool, and mohair. Manufacturers donate fabric and cash awards in each fiber category. And students across the country participate in such national design competitions as Make-It-Yourself with Wool and Suit of the Future. For their best-of-show designs, three Houston Community College fashion design students received the Fashion Group International's top national scholarship awards for study in Paris and London.

At the classroom level, second-year design students at El Centro College in Dallas work one-on-one with local fashion designers, who give the students fabric and ask them for sketches incorporating that fabric. The designers choose which sketches the students will execute, then critique the final product. In New York City, Fashion Institute of Technology (FIT) students participate in such industry-sponsored projects as developing a new fragrance to be sold in a city department store, collaborating with the National Osteoporosis Foundation to design clothing for women with osteoporosis, and creating an advertising campaign for the world's largest sock company.

FIT has the distinction of being the country's first technical school devoted to the apparel industry and counts among its many talented alumni designers

Calvin Klein, Norma Kamali, Jhane Barnes, Mary Ann Restivo, and David Chu. From its inception, the school sought to improve "the compatibility of education and work," in the words of Marvin Feldman, FIT president from 1971 until his retirement in 1992. "We work continuously to erase any difference between what happens in our classrooms and what happens in the industry's workrooms, showrooms, and the marketplace," he said, echoing the objective of other fashion design programs around the country. That real-world focus, encouraged by manufacturers and enjoyed by students, not only fuels the imaginations of future fashion designers but also helps prepare them fully for their profession.

FIT students draw models. Learning to depict the human form is necessary not only for apparel design but also for course study in illustration, life sculpture, and draping—cutting fabric for the best possible fit and drape.

Michael Anthony, a design instructor at El Centro College in Dallas, adjusts a sleeve on the wedding gown he designed for his niece. Second-year design students at El Centro create their own collections, researching trends in the marketplace, sketching 15 pieces, then executing four or five designs for a spring fashion show.

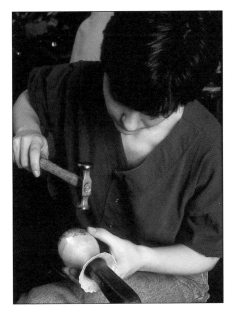

An FIT student in a silversmithing class— a requirement for a degree in jewelry design—gives a small vase a hammered finish. Students become familiar with the properties of metals as they learn to cast and finish pieces in a range of sizes.

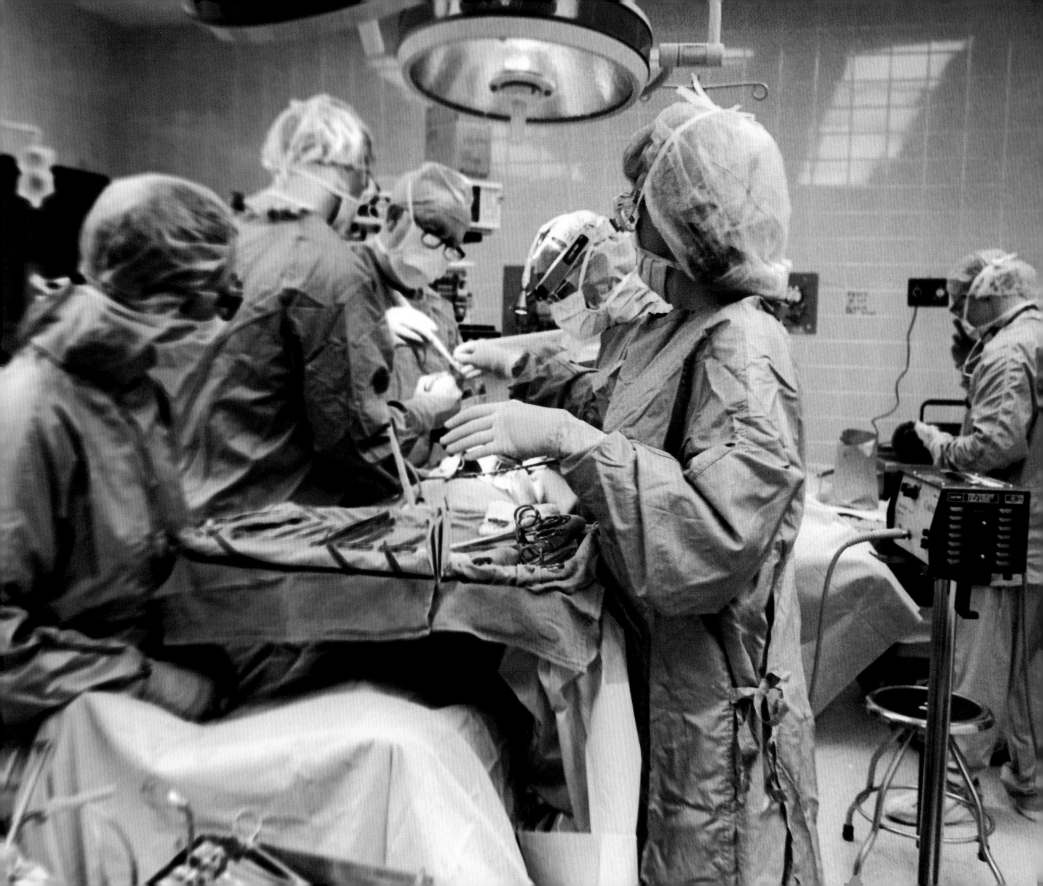

2 Health & Life Sciences

"My family has lived the American dream, made possible by an education system that Illinois Valley Community College is part of."
—*Robert Spetzler, neurosurgeon (Illinois Valley Community College)*

When TWA flight 800 plummeted into the Atlantic off the coast of New York in 1996, nurse Ann Mantel was there counseling relief workers. When southern California was devastated by an earthquake in 1994, she helped residents cope with their losses. Mantel has been on hand to help communities battered by hurricanes and ripped apart by tornadoes. As an American Red Cross volunteer, she has dropped everything and rushed to the site of more than 15 disasters.

Mantel's involvement with the Red Cross goes back almost a quarter of a century, to when she was a nursing student at Jefferson Davis Community College (JDCC) in Alabama. An instructor encouraged students to volunteer to gain hands-on experience, so Mantel signed up to assist with a Red Cross blood drive. Little did she know then what a big part of her life the Red Cross would become. Today, Mantel successfully juggles her job as a nursing instructor at JDCC—she joined

For some students, like biology major Christopher McManus of New York's SUNY Rockland Community College, an associate degree in science is just the beginning of the long process of becoming a doctor or research scientist. Other students enroll in one-year certificate programs with the goal of landing a good job quickly. El Centro College in Texas, for example, prepares students to be operating room technicians (opposite).

Nursing student Tiffany Gonzales (center) explains medications to a mother in a makeshift clinic on the outskirts of Guayaquil, Ecuador, where Gonzales and two members of the nursing faculty at Florida's Hillsborough Community College spent two weeks as part of a medical mission. Their visit was the inspiration for a new course called Transcultural Nursing: Study of Healthcare in an International Setting.

the faculty of her alma mater in 1984—with her volunteer activities. "We have to leave our jobs to give help, and fortunately the college is very supportive of my Red Cross work," Mantel told Alabama's Brewton *Standard.* "That does make a difference when I receive a call asking for help."

Nursing programs were introduced at community colleges in the early 1950s in response to a critical shortage of nurses. Until that time, professional nurses were trained primarily in three-year, hospital-based programs. But these programs became a financial burden for hospitals, and some nurse educators believed the students spent more time doing menial chores than learning nursing competencies. Then Mildred Montag,

a young doctoral student at Columbia University's Teachers College, devised a well-structured curriculum that incorporated clinical experience and prepared nurses in two years instead of three.

States realized that the community college system was the logical place to offer this program, which had the desired effect—a quick infusion of trained nurses into the profession. What developed in the 1950s as a seven-site pilot program has become the norm. Today, some 900 programs offering an associate degree in nursing prepare about 60 percent of the nation's candidates for registered nurse licensing each year.

Nursing and other health professions experienced an increased demand for trained personnel during the

Penn Valley Community College, Missouri, nursing student Michael Adamovich cares for young patient Emori Delphia. Clinical experience is an important part of the nursing program at Penn Valley. Two days a week, students put the skills they learn in the classroom to practical use in medical facilities in the community. Program graduates are eligible to apply to take licensed practical nurse or registered nurse licensing examinations.

Cynthia T. Henderson, an alumna of Chicago's Malcolm X College, made history in 1993 when she was named medical director of Oak Forest Hospital of Cook County. She was the first African American woman and the youngest person ever to be selected.

Beth Kalnins examines a patient at a clinic in Pecatonica, Illinois. Her decision to become a doctor was nurtured at Highland Community College in Illinois. After medical school, Kalnins became a family practice physician with Freeport Health Network.

Michael Caughey credits the "nurturing environment" at Tidewater Community College in Virginia with enabling him to reenter academia following an eight-year absence after high school. Caughey went on to medical school and today is an emergency room physician.

Although Louis Leo's high school counselor told him he "wasn't college material" and he was rejected by 14 nursing schools, Leo was undaunted. From New York's Ulster County Community College he went on to become a physician. He was the fourth doctor in the country to perform balloon angioplasty.

K. Kristene Koontz Gugliuzza, a graduate of Lake Land College in Illinois, directs the Abdominal Transplant Section, University of Texas Medical Branch. She is one of only several dozen female kidney-transplant surgeons in the country, and one of only a handful of women who direct a transplant program.

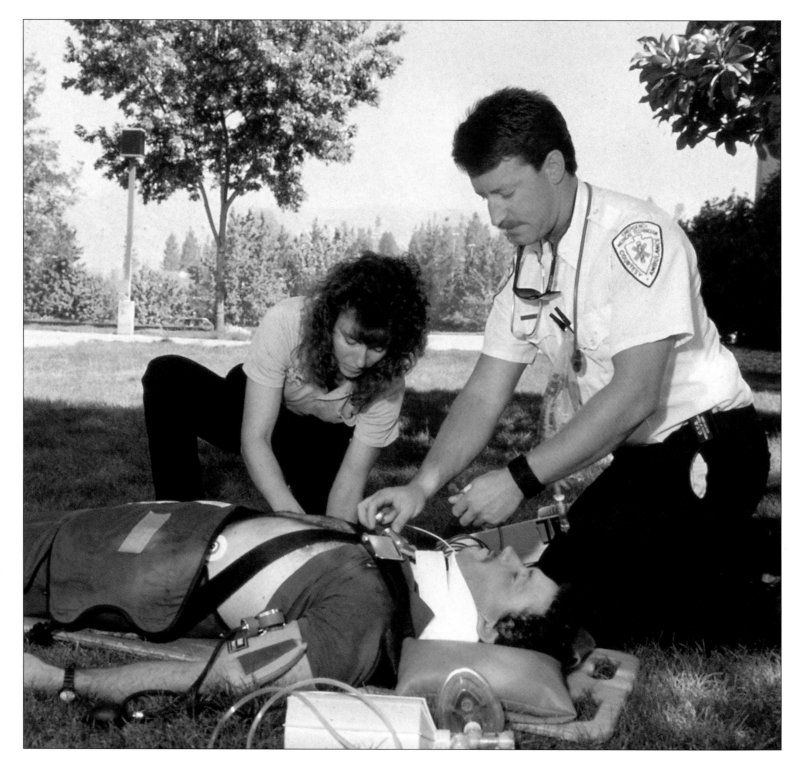

Extensive fieldwork is required of students working toward an associate degree in emergency medical service at California's Crafton Hills College. Here, EMT paramedic students Deborah Strunk and Jamie Wixon practice "stabilizing" classmate Don Martin as part of a simulated emergency care training exercise. For more than 20 years, the college's EMT paramedic program has been the main provider of new paramedics for two California counties.

second half of the 20th century. More associate degrees are awarded in the health professions and related sciences than in any other category except the liberal arts, and about two-thirds of all graduates of health-related community college programs are nurses.

The second-greatest number of health professionals prepared by community colleges are those entering allied health, which encompasses some 200 job categories, including radiography, dental hygiene, medical technology, physical therapy, dietetics, and respiratory therapy. In the past, students entering allied health fields were trained on the job. With staff cutbacks and changes at medical facilities, the responsibility for training has gradually shifted, primarily to community colleges. Today, community colleges educate 65 percent of the nation's new healthcare workers.

Mitch McKee, battalion chief for the City of Redlands Fire Department and a graduate of the emergency medical technical (EMT) paramedic program at California's Crafton Hills College, stresses the need for ongoing training in his field: "Because this is a very

Miami-Dade Community College professors Karen Dillman and Terrence Davis (second and third from left) instruct students of respiratory therapy and emergency medicine using a state-of-the-art "patient" that can take on male or female characteristics and be programmed with more than 200 medical conditions.

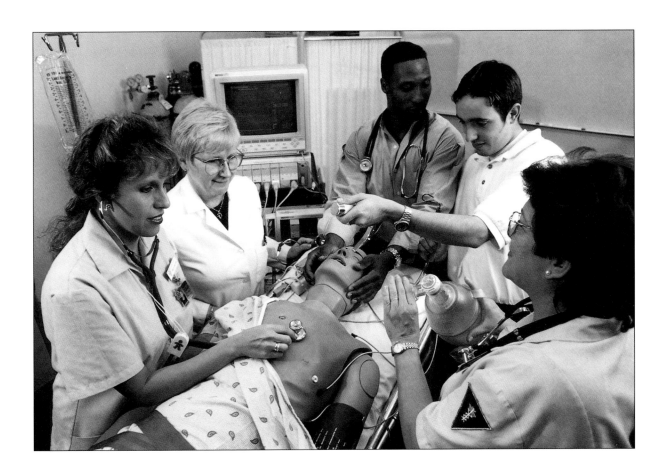

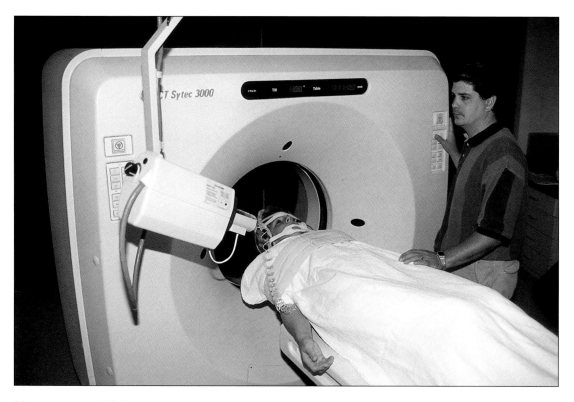

The two-year radiologic technology program at Iowa's Indian Hills Community College works with nearby medical facilities to ensure that students gain experience with the latest equipment. Here, a student operates a magnetic resonance imaging (MRI) machine. More than 65 percent of the program's radiology education is provided in a clinical setting.

Cuauhtemoc Sanchez, *head of hyperbaric medicine at a leading hospital in Mexico City, also directs the Divers Alert Network in Latin America. An expert in what happens to the human body when it is subjected to increased pressure underwater, Sanchez graduated from California's College of Oceaneering, a community college that specializes in training commercial divers and the physicians who treat them.*

dynamic job, continuing education is extremely important. There are constantly new changes in medication, rescue techniques, and equipment." Paramedic training at Crafton Hills includes 164 hours of hospital work and 600 internship hours outside the hospital.

Nursing and allied health programs are particularly important for rural community colleges and may have long waiting lists, because in rural areas a hospital is usually a major employer. By preparing people for a wide range of hospital jobs, the colleges allow residents to stay in the area, which benefits not only the students but local economies.

Community colleges also provide education for front-office employment, including medical record keeping and clerical jobs. These positions, which increasingly require information technology skills, provide essential support to a healthcare structure that serves millions of people each day. Community colleges also prepare students for careers in daycare, mental health, and other human service fields.

Technological advances have had a major impact on healthcare, as evidenced by the growth of such specialized programs as health information technology, biomedical technology, and laser optics. The College of Oceaneering instructs students in the emerging field of hyperbaric medicine, which originated to treat diving problems and has been approved for a number of medical conditions.

With people to apply it, technology can enhance even basic care. Opticianry students at Louisiana's

Students on the College of Oceaneering's diving barge conduct a training drill in which a student simulates decompression illness and will be placed in a hyperbaric chamber. During treatment, the patient breathes 100 percent oxygen through a mask or head tent. Oxygen under pressure helps relieve the patient's symptoms.

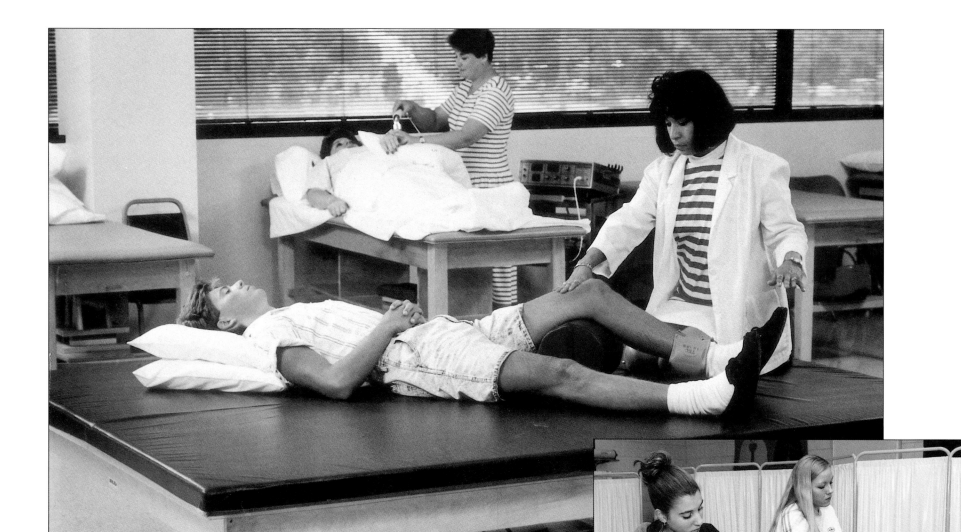

Course work for physical therapist assistants incorporates both academic study and clinical experience, with students performing exercises, massage, traction, and electrical stimulation (above). There are nearly 300 accredited two-year programs for physical therapist assistants in the United States.

Sara DiCenzo and Katherine Hernbeck get some hands-on experience in massage therapy as part of the complementary care program at Berkshire Community College in Massachusetts. When they complete the program, which was introduced at the college in 1998, they will have the skills to become certified massage therapists.

Nunez Community College bring mobile vision screening equipment to community members who otherwise would not have access to it. In partnership with the Louisiana State University Eye Center and the Lions Club, Nunez students make eyeglasses and assist with free screening for schoolchildren and nursing home residents. The innovative service learning program helps students and patients.

Although many community college students choose to begin work as soon as possible, others use a two-year college as the first step in an educational journey that may lead to medical, dental, or veterinary school. Numerous community college graduates have also made significant contributions to their fields through scientific discoveries, medical inventions, and the development of innovative healthcare procedures.

Michael Zanakis, a 1974 graduate of Florida's Indian River Community College, holds more than a dozen patents for medical inventions that have improved the quality of life for people with debilitating spinal cord and other nervous system injuries. The founder of four companies that develop the technologies he invented, Zanakis continues to make advances in his field in his current position as director of research at the Kessler Institute for Rehabilitation in New Jersey. Kessler, the nation's most prestigious medical facility for the care of nervous system injuries, treated actor Christopher Reeve after he sustained paralyzing injuries to his spinal cord in a 1995 horseback riding accident.

Robert Spetzler spoke very little English when he emigrated from Germany in 1954 with his parents and five siblings, but that did not stop him from dreaming of being a neurosurgeon. Spetzler credits his success in part to his local community college. His family's resources were limited, so he opted to study premed at La Salle-Peru-Oglesby Junior College (now Illinois Valley Community College). "My family has lived the American dream, made possible by an education system that IVCC is part of," he says. Spetzler's time at IVCC influenced him greatly and helped give him the confidence he needed to pursue his ambition.

Today, people from all over the world flock to Spetzler's Arizona practice, primarily to take advantage of a surgical technique he pioneered. "Standstill" brain surgery is said to improve surgical outcomes and shorten recovery time. The patient is placed in a deep coma to reduce the amount of oxygen the brain needs. The heart is stopped, the brain is chilled, and the blood is drained from the body while the neurosurgeon operates. Columnist Jimmy Breslin underwent the procedure when Spetzler removed an aneurysm from his brain. Breslin wrote about the experience and related that he was back to work just days after the delicate operation.

Cancer research has also benefited from the dedication of a number of community college graduates. John

The Chicago Bulls and the Golden State Warriors are just two of the professional sports teams that have benefited from the skills of **Donald Chu,** *a physical therapist and expert on fitness and athletic training. A graduate of Ohlone College in California, Chu returned to his alma mater in 1997 as director of its physical therapist assistant program. He is an author, popular speaker, and radio personality in his home state of California.*

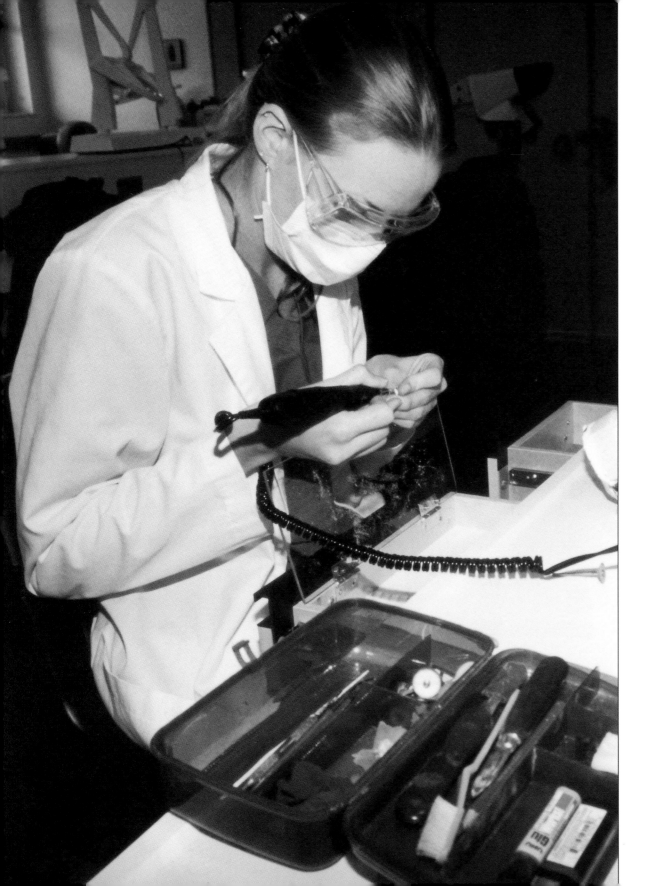

Michael Pezzuto, a graduate of Atlantic Cape Community College in New Jersey and now a respected cancer researcher at the University of Illinois at Chicago, studies how the world's plants and other natural resources can be used to develop new generations of chemotherapy drugs.

Molecular biologist and genetic researcher Elaine A. Ostrander, who earned an associate in science degree at Yakima Valley Community College in Washington before continuing her studies, made headlines across the country with her research findings. In 1996, she announced that women—especially those of European Jewish descent—with no family history of breast cancer were likely to get the disease before age 35 if they had defects in a specific gene that normally protects against tumor growth. Ostrander is researching similar genes that predispose men to inherited prostate cancer.

Community colleges provide an opportunity for students to pursue their interests, even if their life goals take time to emerge. Shirley Johnson loved animals and wanted to work with them, but she could not afford to go away to college. Then she heard about the veterinary technology program at the Loudoun campus of Northern Virginia Community College (NVCC). Even before graduating, Johnson had the promise of a job at the nearby Reston Animal Park. In the next 18 years, Johnson married the owner of the park, raised a family, and continued caring for the animals. She hosts occasional classes of vet tech students from NVCC who

Student Crissie Taylor practices what she has learned in the dental lab technology program at Indian River Community College in Florida. Students put their new skills to use by making bridges, crowns, and other dental appliances for patients in the college's dental clinic, which is open to the public.

come to the park for hands-on experience with exotic animals. And at age 38, Johnson at last applied to veterinary school, taking another step toward a goal that had come into sharp focus in the years since her graduation from NVCC.

Many community college students find a way to pursue their dreams and to help others, as evidenced by Karen Kay Medville, a member of the Cherokee Nation who grew up in a rural mining community in Colorado. Medville had few economic or educational advantages, and soon after graduating from high school she found herself in desperate straits—on welfare with a baby daughter. She knew she had to do something to provide a future for her child. While driving through Colorado Springs one day, she heard a radio ad for Pikes Peak Community College (PPCC). She made the decision then and there to sell all her household belongings and move to Colorado Springs.

Medville enrolled at PPCC and immediately felt at home. Her self-esteem soared. "I got good grades and discovered that I really could learn. People were gen-

Dennis Lynch (left) and James Gauer are two of the first graduates of the optical systems technology program at Monroe Community College in New York. The program, the first of its kind in the country, prepares graduates to work alongside scientists and engineers in high-technology fields that employ light and optical principles.

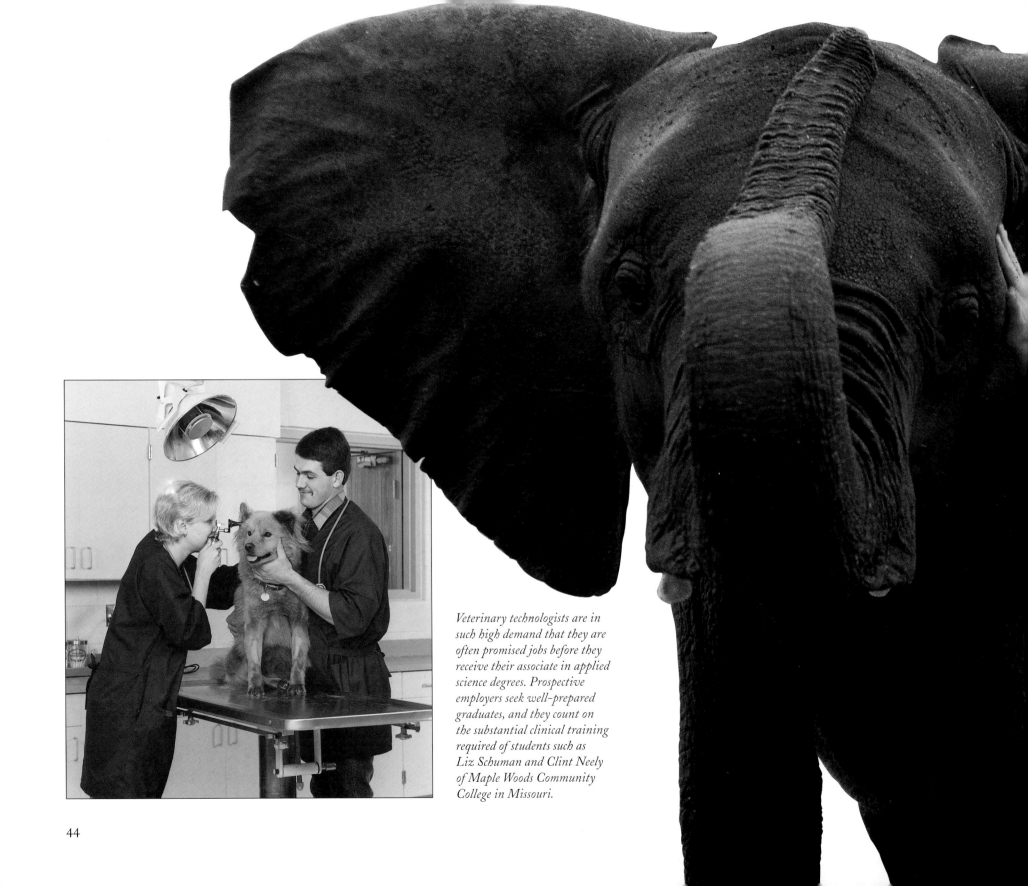

Veterinary technologists are in such high demand that they are often promised jobs before they receive their associate in applied science degrees. Prospective employers seek well-prepared graduates, and they count on the substantial clinical training required of students such as Liz Schuman and Clint Neely of Maple Woods Community College in Missouri.

44

uinely happy for you when you succeeded," she recalled. In 1982, she graduated with an associate in science degree in biology and chemistry. But that was just the beginning of her education. Medville credits the faculty at PPCC with inspiring her to further her education. She went on to earn a bachelor's degree in biology, a master's in physiology and biophysics, and a doctorate from Cornell University in environmental toxicology. She then joined the faculty of Arizona State University West in Phoenix, where she researches the effects of environmental toxins—such as lead and copper—that people encounter in their communities and on the job. She is an inspiration to Native American youth and often speaks to them about her successes as a scientist.

Medville has not forgotten the pivotal role her community college experience played in her life. Every summer for five weeks and throughout the school year, she opens up her lab to disadvantaged minority youth enrolled in community colleges. Her goal is to inspire them and get them excited about science, with the hope that they will continue their education after they earn their associate degrees. She says, "I want them to see me as a role model, someone who was once in the same situation as they are but who overcame my disadvantages. I tell them that if I could do it then they can do it."

Sukari, a big-eared African elephant, is shown with owner Shirley Johnson, a 1981 graduate of the veterinary technology program at Northern Virginia Community College. Johnson and her husband own an exotic animal farm near the college's Loudoun campus, making it an ideal field-trip destination for vet tech students looking for hands-on experience.

NORTHERN MAINE TECHNICAL COLLEGE

SOUTHERN MAINE TECHNICAL COLLEGE

UNIVERSITY OF MAINE AT AUGUSTA *Two-Year Branch Campus*

WASHINGTON COUNTY TECHNICAL COLLEGE

YORK COUNTY TECHNICAL COLLEGE

MARYLAND

ALLEGANY COLLEGE OF MARYLAND

ANNE ARUNDEL COMMUNITY COLLEGE

BALTIMORE CITY COMMUNITY COLLEGE

BALTIMORE INTERNATIONAL COLLEGE

CARROLL COMMUNITY COLLEGE

CECIL COMMUNITY COLLEGE

CHESAPEAKE COLLEGE

COLLEGE OF SOUTHERN MARYLAND

COMMUNITY COLLEGE OF BALTIMORE COUNTY

COMMUNITY COLLEGE OF BALTIMORE COUNTY —CATONSVILLE —DUNDALK —ESSEX

FREDERICK COMMUNITY COLLEGE

GARRETT COMMUNITY COLLEGE

HAGERSTOWN COMMUNITY COLLEGE

HARFORD COMMUNITY COLLEGE

The Media

"IF THERE HAD NOT BEEN A TYLER JUNIOR COLLEGE, I AM QUITE SURE THAT
I WOULD NEVER HAVE GOTTEN TO COLLEGE."
                    —Sarah McClendon, White House correspondent (Tyler Junior College, Texas)

Not only did Tyler Junior College in Texas provide news correspondent Sarah McClendon with an avenue to higher education, it also pointed her toward her future career. Looking back at her most memorable experiences at Tyler, the veteran journalist remembered Miss Lillian Howell, languages and drama instructor, "pointing her finger at me one day and saying, 'You, Sarah McClendon, will go to the University of Missouri School of Journalism and learn to be a reporter.'" Until that moment, recalled McClendon, "I had not thought about it."

Not all journalists and others in communications have a Miss Howell to thank for guiding them. But many credit community college courses in journalism, television and radio broadcasting, photography, and other areas with fueling their interest in various media. For Jim Lehrer, anchor of the Public Broadcasting System's *NewsHour with Jim Lehrer,* "It was while I was a student at Victoria College that I truly decided journalism and writing were for me. I was the editor of the student newspaper, a job that provided me an opportunity to report, write, and edit a little bit of everything."

At Miami–Dade Community College, students in television and video production courses practice their skills behind and in front of the camera. The news broadcast set was donated by the local CBS affiliate. At left, an aspiring producer.

Jim Lehrer, a graduate of Victoria College in Texas, is executive editor and anchor of The NewsHour with Jim Lehrer on PBS. A reporter since 1959, Lehrer has won two Emmys and in 1999 was inducted into the Television Hall of Fame.

Herb Caen, a Sacramento City College alumnus and beloved columnist for the San Francisco Chronicle until his death at the age of 80 in 1997, wrote a daily column for 58 years— longer than anyone else in U.S. news- paper history.

Freelance correspondent Sarah McClendon was a member of the first graduating class of Tyler Junior College in 1928. A news analyst, lecturer, and author, the veteran reporter has covered 11 presidents since she was assigned the White House beat in June 1944.

A 1977 graduate of Northampton Community College in Pennsylvania, photographer Carol Guzy won the first of three Pulitzer Prizes in 1986, the first female photojournalist to win the award. "It's the people in the pictures and those who view them that are important," she says.

Managing editor of the Seattle Post-Intelligencer since 1993, Kenneth Bunting, an alumnus of Lee College in Texas, participated in a national task force that rewrote accreditation standards for colleges and universities in 1983.

An advocate for missing and exploited children since the murder of his own son in 1981, John Walsh, a graduate of New York's Cayuga County Community College, hosts Fox Television's America's Most Wanted.

From his seat in the studio at SUNY Rockland Community College in New York, Anthony Solin records a radio program. Students at the college can take advantage of internships in New York City and throughout the region, and a course called Broadcasting in Britain offers an opportunity to study abroad.

A student at Waldorf College in Iowa broadcasts from the sound booth at KZOW Radio. The first student-managed, fully digital radio station in the country, KZOW debuted in September 1995. Communications students at Waldorf complete two internships and have the opportunity to study in Oxford, England, in conjunction with their major.

Other community college students pursued their early dreams only to change careers later. John Walsh, a liberal arts major at Auburn (now Cayuga County) Community College in New York, is host of the Fox Television show *America's Most Wanted* and a leading advocate for missing and exploited children. Pulitzer Prize-winning photographer Carol Guzy received her associate degree in nursing from Northampton Community College in Pennsylvania before deciding to pursue photography as a career. It was the nursing program, she said, that "helped me gain an understanding of human suffering and an incredible sensitivity to it. I know that without this background, my photography would have a totally different edge."

For every highly visible journalist, there are many community college graduates working behind the scenes as camera operators, lighting technicians, and

producers. Some entered a studio for the first time during broadcast courses like those at New York's Herkimer County Community College. There, second-year television students learn to produce their own shows, shooting a short feature or taping an interview that airs over a public access channel. They also serve as crew for campus television shows. Radio students work at the campus station as news, music, and sports directors, and some take a seat behind the microphone—their first step, perhaps, toward becoming on-air personalities.

Students at New York's Herkimer County Community College set up operations in the mobile video production van, which allows them to broadcast live events. Students get hands-on experience shooting athletic contests and such off-campus events as city council meetings, which air live over the college's public access channel.

Business & Industry

"At some point, there's a light that goes on that says, 'We're going to make a difference.'"

—*Bruce FaBrizio, Sunshine Makers, Inc. (Mt. San Antonio Community College, California)*

When Georgia's New Ebenezer College opened its doors in January 1887, one of its goals, as described in its first catalog, was to "prepare pupils for business." Now known as Middle Georgia College, this institution and community colleges across the country remain true to that mission. They not only prepare students to step into jobs in a variety of businesses, but also equip people to start and run their own companies.

Bennye Dickerson *(left)* of Arlington, Texas, is one of the many entrepreneurs who have emerged from a community college. In 1997, Dickerson was on disabil-ity leave from her nursing job when she decided to attend her local college to learn about owning a business. Now she's her own boss, designing, manufacturing, and marketing a line of African American-inspired clothing and accessories for infants and children.

The 53-year-old grandmother of 13 had created unique designs for family and friends for years. Acting on their encouragement, Dickerson finally decided to go into business. Through the Technology Assistance Center at the Dallas County Community College District's Bill J. Priest Institute, she received career coun-

Students practice their typing skills on manual typewriters at Northeast Wisconsin Technical College in the early 1960s. Other business courses popular before the computer era included shorthand dictation and ledger bookkeeping.

Preparing for a career in customer service, Edward Bullock practices responding to inquiries at the Ameritech Call Center training facility at Ohio's Cuyahoga Community College. The center was created to help fill the need for qualified professionals at 60,000 call centers across the nation.

A student in the professional crafts program at Haywood Community College in North Carolina learns the art of weaving. The program— which includes specialties in clay, fiber, jewelry, and wood—emphasizes entrepreneurship. Students study the finer points of how to start and run a small business.

Kirti Valia works in a lab at Core Tech Solutions, Inc., one of more than 50 businesses nurtured in the High Technology Small Business Incubator at Burlington County College in New Jersey. Core Tech develops transdermal and transmucosal drug delivery systems for pharmaceutical companies.

seling and legal advice. She identified a potential market of 39 million customers, test-marketed her products, and attended trade shows to link up with retailers. With the aid of her counselors, Dickerson negotiated licensing and royalty agreements. After only 15 months with the center, she solicited and won a lucrative JCPenney account; her products are now offered for sale in selected stores. As her company grows, Dickerson hopes to create jobs in her community, hiring business students to help with manufacturing and sales. Community college "is a wonderful place for people like myself who don't know how to go about breaking into business," Dickerson told the *Dallas Morning News.* "They'll help you all the way down the line."

Roughly two-thirds of all new jobs and half of all new inventions in the United States are generated by small business. Two-year institutions across the country have instituted "business incubators" to give new small businesses the technical support and access to expertise that are essential for success.

Burlington County College's Mount Laurel campus in New Jersey is home to the High Technology Small Business Incubator, which hosts businesses ranging from high-tech pharmaceutical companies to multimedia and Web site providers. The incubator helps startup companies develop, manufacture, and market their goods and services, and as the businesses become self-sufficient, they leave to be replaced by other startups. In just two years, the incubator has had three "graduates" and now assists more than 50 young businesses. Startups receive low-cost office and lab space, access to a variety of business-planning services, and technical support from faculty members and local, state, and federal agencies.

Helping small businesses succeed has also been the mission of the Milwaukee Enterprise Center (MEC).

Through a partnership that includes the city, the state of Wisconsin, and Milwaukee Area Technical College, MEC has served as its community's small business incubator since 1986. Among the businesses currently occupying MEC's 190,000-square-foot building are a robotics assembly and engineering firm, a food and beverage

Bruce FaBrizio, graduate of California's Mt. San Antonio Community College, put his passion and business acumen to work developing Simple Green, a household and industrial cleaner that is part of an environmentally friendly product line. FaBrizio has donated products from his company, Sunshine Makers, Inc., to promote the use of nontoxic chemicals for the safety of people and the environment.

Dennis Craig Curry distinguished himself in the insurance field as president of Signature Insurance Group, Inc., a firm with $20 million in annual sales. A 1968 graduate of Central Florida Community College in Ocala, Curry has also served as the city's mayor and as a council member.

"*Your objective should be excellence,*" advises **Michael Duff**, *a trial attorney with the National Labor Relations Board in Philadelphia. Duff, who came from a working-class background, graduated in 1980 from Pennsylvania's Delaware County Community College; his impressive academic achievements eventually led to a degree from Harvard Law School. He believes "there is no one way of getting where you want to be. The key is to keep moving and to generate options."*

Herbert Hafif *graduated in 1951 from California's Chaffey College and had earned his first million dollars in various business ventures before receiving his law degree from the University of Southern California. By successfully combining business and law, Hafif has founded more than a dozen corporations, ranging from sewer and pipeline construction companies to restaurants to real estate development firms.*

Mary Ann Stiles, *a graduate of Hillsborough Community College in Florida, is now a partner in a law firm that specializes in workers' compensation, regulatory, corporate, and government law. Stiles has published several books on workers' compensation and has represented the business community before the legislature for more than 20 years. She is a past chair of Hillsborough's board of trustees.*

distributor, a computerized office services provider, and a production knitting mill. Tenants receive technical training and consultation in finance and other critical aspects of business, and they enjoy the benefits of bulk discounts on office supplies and equipment, advertising, and group health insurance.

Although accounting, marketing, and office systems programs enroll the greatest number of community college business students, nearly every college offers an array of business courses. These might include credit and noncredit courses, courses delivered through distance learning methods, programs developed in collaboration with industry, or internships with accounting or law firms. For many large companies, forming an alliance with community colleges makes sound business sense. Organized training centers and educational programs help ensure the quality and quantity of workers to keep U.S. businesses competitive. Chairman of the Federal Reserve Alan Greenspan commented during a Senate committee hearing that "the value of on-the-job-training and the remarkable expansion in community colleges [have] had a major positive effect on our workforce," an acknowledgment of community colleges' role as a provider of well-prepared workers for business and industry.

Some partnerships reach beyond the boundaries of one country and can result in unexpected benefits.

A business faculty member at Colorado's Aims Community College helps a student choose from suits and dresses in the college's professional clothing bank. Students who need clothing appropriate for job interviews turn to the bank, which stocks donated outfits. To the same end, Dallas County instructor Juanita Marquez used a classroom closet to start her Unique Boutique, a collection of donated interview attire for women and men.

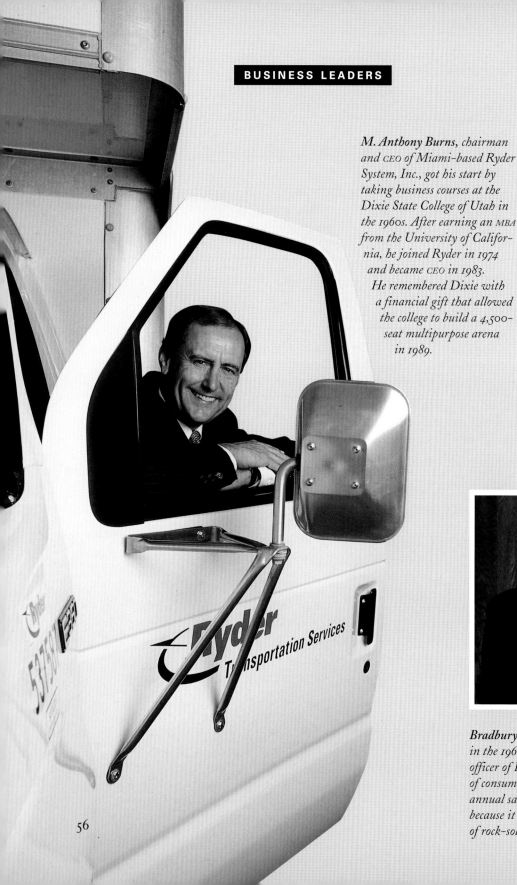

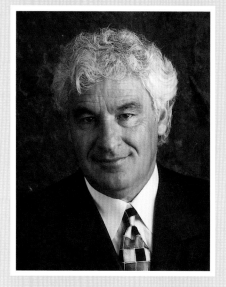

M. Anthony Burns, chairman and CEO *of Miami-based Ryder System, Inc., got his start by taking business courses at the Dixie State College of Utah in the 1960s. After earning an* MBA *from the University of California, he joined Ryder in 1974 and became* CEO *in 1983. He remembered Dixie with a financial gift that allowed the college to build a 4,500-seat multipurpose arena in 1989.*

In 1971, when he was only 30 years old, **Thomas Golisano,** *a graduate of* SUNY *College of Technology-Alfred, founded Paychex, Inc., with just $3,000. Today the billion-dollar firm provides payroll and human resources services, especially to small and medium-sized businesses.*

Anne Elizabeth Nelson, a senior vice president at Salomon Smith Barney, studied business at the Community College of Vermont in the 1980s. Since then, she has risen to the top of her field and was named one of 1998's "best brokers" by On Wall Street magazine.

Business skills fostered at Ontario's Seneca College in the 1970s propelled **Valerio Azzoli** *to the top post at legendary Atlantic Records. In 1990, Azzoli began a strategic revamping of the firm, and by the end of the decade, annual revenues had increased to more than $700 million.*

Bradbury Anderson *attended Iowa's Waldorf College in the 1960s. Now he is president and chief operating officer of Best Buy, the nation's number one retailer of consumer electronics, with more than $7 billion in annual sales. Says Anderson, "Waldorf worked for me because it inspired a love of learning in a community of rock-solid values."*

War II before joining the Bendix Field Engineering Corporation. By 1962, he had become president of the 4,000-employee company, a position he held until his retirement in 1970. His company provided launch support for the successful *Apollo 11* mission in 1969.

In the 1960s, Gerald Howard Gordon drove a newspaper delivery truck for the Cleveland *Plain Dealer*. Just after midnight, his route would take him past Cuyahoga Community College. He longed to enroll but lacked the courage, until one day, Gordon recalled, "I made up my mind there was no way I could do 43 more years in the middle of the night on that truck."

Taking his future in his hands, Gordon enrolled at the college in 1964. After more than seven years of night school, he had earned not only his associate degree from Cuyahoga but also his bachelor's and master's degrees from Cleveland State University. Gordon went to work for Sun Newspapers in 1973 and was named general manager just four years later. From 1973 through

Johnson County Community College in Kansas is home to the National Academy of Railroad Sciences, offering courses in pre-engineering, civil engineering, technology, drafting, and railroad operations. A simulated cab built with controls and hydraulics creates full train motion. Academy director Andy Burton calls the railroad industry "alive and well" and anticipates a growing need for academy graduates as railroads lose employees to retirement.

Billy Johnson and Stan Lyles, students in the residential construction program at Cossatot Technical College in Arkansas, adjust roof beams. The house they are working on is a joint project between the college and the local rural development authority and will go on the market when completed. Proceeds will help fund the college's scholarship program for building trades students.

1979, Gordon also taught part-time at Cuyahoga, sharing with students the same enthusiasm for learning that had inspired him. Gordon is now president and chief operating officer of SunMedia Group, whose Sun Newspapers division is the largest chain of suburban weeklies in the country. Although Gordon left teaching to concentrate on business, since 1993 he has served on the Ohio Board of Regents, where he helps set the state's higher education policies.

At age 19, Richard M. Scrushy was a husband and father attending night classes at Alabama's Jefferson State Community College to earn an associate in science degree. Scrushy went on to teach respiratory therapy and started respiratory therapy departments at two community colleges before going into health management. He founded and now serves as CEO and chairman of the board of Health-

South Corporation, a healthcare company with more than 2,000 facilities internationally.

For Scrushy, the flexibility offered by community college was key. For a father working his way through school, "the ability to wrap the community college around my schedule was everything." He credits his instructors with instilling important skills: "I learned so much from the people who taught me. They taught me how to teach. That's what management is all about, because a teacher is like a manager. It's all about communication and leadership."

Students at Catawba Valley Community College in North Carolina learn upholstery skills in the college's furniture production lab. Students may earn a certificate in upholstery or upholstery pattern making, or they may pursue an associate in applied science degree in furniture production technology or design and product development.

*Born in Colombia, **Juan C. Guerra** arrived in the United States in 1979. He graduated from Central Florida Community College with an associate degree in engineering and went on to earn a master's in structural engineering from the University of Florida. He is now chairman of Guerra Development Corporation, a consulting engineering firm.*

A Winning Spirit

"South Plains prepared me for Division 1 classes and Division 1 basketball."
—*Sheryl Swoopes, Olympic gold medalist (South Plains College, Texas)*

Ray Bartlett remembers that his long-time friend and teammate Jackie Robinson first received wide recognition for his extraordinary athletic talent while attending Pasadena Junior College (now Pasadena City College), where Robinson and Bartlett lettered in football, basketball, baseball, and track from 1937 to 1939. Bartlett continued to catch Robinson's "wobbly passes"—his strength was running—on the football team at the University of California, Los Angeles, where Robinson lettered in four sports and Bartlett in three.

Of all the games and sports they played together, Bartlett remembers playing football together at Pasadena as the most fun. "We had such a good team at Pasadena Junior College," Bartlett said, "we just walked away with the conference championship."

Robinson went on to win the World Series and awards like Rookie of the Year and Most Valuable Player in baseball, but his most historic feat was breaking the major league color barrier as a Brooklyn Dodger in 1947. Matthew "Mack" Robinson—Jackie's brother and fellow Pasadena student—made history at the 1936 Olympics in Berlin as one of 10 African Americans to win 14 medals at the games clouded by Hitler's racism. Mack won silver in the 200-meter dash. College of San Mateo graduate Archie Williams won a gold medal in the 400-meter race at the same Olympics.

Bernadette Mattox, head women's basketball coach at the University of Kentucky, says the friendships she made at Roane State Community College in Tennessee helped build her confidence to play basketball and coach at the collegiate level. Mattox earned all-American honors at the University of Georgia and in 1990 became the first female assistant coach of a Division 1 men's basketball team.

Kevin Saunders credits Del Mar College, Texas, with turning his life around after a grain-elevator explosion left him paralyzed. Saunders says his Del Mar classes "helped my mind respond to an overwhelming, horrific situation," and were "the basis of all the things I've been able to accomplish." Saunders, a Paralympic medalist, was named Best All Around Wheelchair Athlete in the World from 1990 to 1992.

Western Maryland's mountains, Deep Creek Lake, and Savage River provide spectacular classrooms for the adventure-sports program at Garrett Community College. Noncredit outdoor enthusiasts and associate degree students majoring in adventuresports may choose from more than 40 adventure skill courses.

Hinds Community College hurdler Wenston Riley achieved National Junior College Athletic Association (NJCAA) All-American honors twice in indoor and outdoor track. Track is one of 11 scholarship sports at Hinds, which has five times won the prestigious Halbrook Award, given to Mississippi colleges and universities that graduate a high percentage of athletes.

Indian River Community College swimmers have the longest winning streak in the nation. The men's team has won the NJCAA Swimming and Diving Championship 26 years in a row, from 1975 to 2000; the women's team has won the championship 22 times since 1976. All-American Jamie McCarthy contributed to The River's winning legacy during the 1998 and 1999 seasons.

The Robinson brothers and Williams are just three of the world-class athletes community colleges claim as their own. Thousands of former students have distinguished themselves in professional sports. Numerous community college athletes have been on Olympic teams as well. Although many superstars attended community college because they were recruited, many were drawn to their alma maters for the same reason millions of other students enroll: The colleges offer high-quality postsecondary education close to home.

Homesickness prompted women's basketball star and Olympic gold medalist Sheryl Swoopes to abandon a university scholarship. When she got home she called Lyndon Hardin, the women's basketball coach at nearby South Plains College, Texas, to find out if it was too late to join his team. Hardin thought it was a prank until Swoopes showed up at the gym. At South Plains, Swoopes scored a record 1,555 points, earned her associate degree, and was a two-time National Junior College Athletic Association All-American. Swoopes says Hardin played a major role in her collegiate and professional success. "He didn't just care about me as an athlete, he cared about me as a person. That was important to me," Swoopes said, adding that "South Plains prepared me for Division 1 classes and Division 1 basketball."

Famed pitcher Nolan Ryan went right from high school to the major leagues, so he attended Alvin Community College in his Texas hometown during the off season. "It enabled not only me but my wife to come

Josh Parrish blasts past a goalie to score for Kansas's Johnson County Community College in 1997. One of the team's top producers, Parrish made 36 goals in two years. Soccer has been popular at community colleges since the 1950s. The NJCAA held its first national soccer championship in 1961.

Archie Williams of California's College of San Mateo won a gold medal at the 1936 Olympics in Berlin by running 400 meters in 46.5 seconds. His was one of 14 medals won by African American athletes whose success refuted Hitler's racism. After a military career, Williams taught high school math and coached track in San Anselmo, California.

Cathy Turner *races toward her second Olympic gold medal (right) and a world record in 500-meter speed skating at the 1994 Olympics in Lillehammer, Norway. She won the same event at the 1992 Olympics, making her one of the few to win gold medals in consecutive Winter Olympics. Turner is a graduate of New York's Monroe Community College.*

OLYMPIANS

Cynthia Ann Gettinger won gold medals in freestyle, backstroke, breaststroke, and butterfly swimming at the 1988 Paralympics in Seoul. The Manatee Community College, Florida, graduate appreciated college personnel, who challenged students "no matter who you were."

Dionna M. Harris *led the first U.S. Olympic softball team to a gold medal with a .409 batting average during the Atlanta Games in 1996. The Delaware Technical and Community College graduate is the first Delaware woman and only the second Delaware resident to win an Olympic gold medal.*

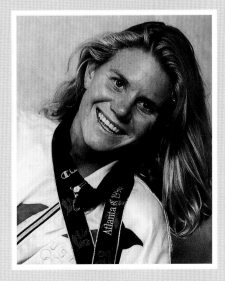

Pete Rademacher, a 1956 Olympic gold medalist in boxing, began his pro career fighting champ Floyd Patterson. He didn't win, but his determination helped the Yakima Valley Community College alumnus succeed in other bouts, and later as an inventor and businessman.

During his incredible 27-year major league pitching career, **Nolan Ryan** was known for his fastball and endurance. He pitched seven no-hit games, 12 one-hit games, struck out 5,714 batters, and won 324 games. The National Baseball Hall of Fame inducted the former Alvin Community College student in 1999.

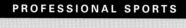

PROFESSIONAL SPORTS

Pitcher **Jaime Navarro** won more than 100 major league games after leaving Miami-Dade Community College's Wolfson campus. He shows his appreciation for a baseball scholarship by hosting a celebrity golf tournament to benefit the college's athletic programs.

Long before she was an international leader in women's basketball, **Sheryl Swoopes** (right) played at South Plains College, Texas. Swoopes won a gold medal with her teammates at the 1996 and 2000 Olympics and is one of the top players in the Women's National Basketball Association.

During his 30 years as National Football League commissioner, **Pete Rozelle**, a graduate of California's Compton Community College, oversaw the merger with the American Football League and helped make football highly profitable.

Jackie Robinson starred on the baseball, football, basketball, and track teams at Pasadena Junior College from 1937 to 1939. In his autobiography, Robinson recounts a happy day in 1938 when he set a running broad jump record in the morning and played shortstop in the baseball championship Pasadena won in the afternoon. In 1947, Robinson became the first African American to play major league baseball.

Mitch Richmond played a record 78 games between 1984 and 1986 at Moberly Area Community College, Missouri. He was NBA Rookie of the Year in 1988-89, and Most Valuable Player in the 1995 All-Star Game. He also played on the 1988 and 1996 U.S. Olympic teams.

back in the off season," Ryan explained, "to work and to attend college at the same time in our area." Ruth Ryan now serves as a college trustee. For 17 years, Ryan hosted ACC's celebrity golf tournament. His foundation gave more than $1 million for a continuing education and community center, a portion of which houses an exhibit on Ryan's career that attracts thousands of tourists annually. An interactive display lets visitors feel what it is like to catch Ryan's legendary fastball.

Two-time Olympic gold medalist Cathy Turner completed her associate degree in data processing during a hiatus in her speed skating career. "Monroe Community College helped me with a great educational base, so anywhere I went, traveling and for my sports, I was able to pop into a school and transfer my credits."

Though more than half of the nation's nearly 1,200 associate degree-granting institutions offer intercolle-giate programs for students to continue playing the sports they love, community colleges have also broadened participation in athletics by emphasizing lifelong fitness and wellness for all students. Programs from kayaking to water exercise extend the educational experience beyond the classroom to help students find creative outlets for their physical and mental talents.

The inclusive attitude of community colleges has made them welcoming places for disabled athletes as well. World champion wheelchair athlete Kevin Saunders, the first person with a disability to serve on the President's Council on Physical Fitness and Sports, says Del Mar College was instrumental in his recovery from paralyzing injuries he suffered in an explosion. "I was inspired by the way my mind...responded to my studies and the rebuilding of my body," he said. He now shares his inspiration as a motivational speaker.

*Four-time world champion steer wrestler **Ote Berry** was selected for the Pro Rodeo Hall of Fame in 1998. Berry participated on Eastern Wyoming College's rodeo team, then hit his stride after graduation on the professional rodeo circuit, where only the winners get paid. Roping, riding, and wrestling uncooperative animals appeals to many at the 135 colleges and universities that belong to the National Intercollegiate Rodeo Association. Eastern Wyoming has had a rodeo team for 25 years. In 2000, 60 men and women participated.*

JEFFERSON COMMUNITY COLLEGE

KINGSBOROUGH COMMUNITY COLLEGE

LABORATORY INSTITUTE OF MERCHANDISING

LAGUARDIA COMMUNITY COLLEGE

MARIA COLLEGE

MATER DEI COLLEGE

MOHAWK VALLEY COMMUNITY COLLEGE

MONROE COLLEGE

MONROE COMMUNITY COLLEGE

NASSAU COMMUNITY COLLEGE

NIAGARA COUNTY COMMUNITY COLLEGE

NORTH COUNTRY COMMUNITY COLLEGE

ONONDAGA COMMUNITY COLLEGE

ORANGE COUNTY COMMUNITY COLLEGE

PAUL SMITH'S COLLEGE OF ARTS AND SCIENCES

QUEENSBOROUGH COMMUNITY COLLEGE

ROCHESTER INSTITUTE OF TECHNOLOGY— NATIONAL TECHNICAL INSTITUTE FOR THE DEAF

SAGE JUNIOR COLLEGE OF ALBANY

SCHENECTADY COUNTY COMMUNITY COLLEGE

SUFFOLK COUNTY COMMUNITY COLLEGE

SULLIVAN COUNTY COMMUNITY COLLEGE

4 *Public & Community Service*

"ANYTHING CAN BE ACCESSIBLE, WITH AN ACCESSIBLE MIND."

—*Foster Andersen, founder of Shared Adventures (Monroe Community College, New York)*

Community colleges teach the importance of active government, public, and community service. Through service learning (classroom learning combined with course-relevant community service), volunteering, holding public office, and responsibly advocating social change, community college instructors, students, and alumni donate their time and energy to renew their communities. In Michigan, the Black Student Association at Jackson Community College has undertaken such projects as cleaning up local neighborhoods *(left)*. Building trades students at Iowa Western Community College have used their skills to make a local nature trail wheelchair-accessible and to construct houses with Habitat for Humanity.

For those who consider the global community their home and who strive to promote renewal in other parts of the world, two instructors at Wisconsin's Northcentral Technical College (NTC) offer leadership by example. Marjorie Bock and Kristin Van Der Geest and their students build solar cookers, which use heat from the sun to boil water or cook food—a boon to those in poverty-stricken countries who cannot afford tradition-

In a Honduran town where fuel is scarce, Northcentral Technical College instructors Marjorie Bock (in sunglasses) and Kristin Van Der Geest teach residents how to use a solar cooker. Van Der Geest realized "the tremendous impact these simple cookers could make" when the Hondurans thanked God for this "miracle."

Miss America 1996, Shawntel Smith—a graduate of Westark College in Arkansas—spent her year in the spotlight advocating school-to-work programs that help prepare students for high-skill careers. "Young people need help in making the transition from the classroom to the workplace," she told the Los Angeles Times. "They rely on us to help them make a difference."

Northern Virginia Community College president Belle Wheelan talks with students at the fall 1998 grand opening of NVCC's Head Start program on the Alexandria campus. The college offers a free educational program for Head Start parents, who learn parenting and computer skills while strengthening their English.

al heating and cooking fuels. In 1999, the NTC Foundation awarded the two women $2,500 for exemplary service. They used the award to travel to Honduras, where they taught villagers to build the cookers and helped set up a solar-cooker distribution center. "The gratitude of the people when we were able to help them was just incredible," Bock recalled later. The two instructors believe the program enhances the lives of the students who build the cookers as well as those of the recipients. Said Bock, "Each student benefits by giving back to the community at large."

Eula Miller also knows the rewards of establishing an innovative program. Miller heads the early childhood education program at Northern Virginia Community College's Alexandria campus. The program collaborates with NVCC's Community and Workforce Development department, Alexandria's Head Start, and the human services organization the Campagna Center to provide an educational and support program for Head Start children's parents. The program includes training in English and basic computer skills and works to enhance parenting skills. As Miller says, "Every time you help a parent, you make it better for a child."

Community college students, faculty, and alumni often work to help others. Many, including alumnus Foster Andersen, had to overcome personal hardship first. In 1978, a serious motorcycle accident left Andersen unable to walk. Yet, he was determined to find a way to enjoy the outdoor adventures he loved. After graduating from New York's Monroe Community Col-

Kweisi Mfume, a graduate of Baltimore City Community College, earned wide respect as a civil rights leader, city councilman, and congressman. In 1996, he became president and CEO of the NAACP.

In 1993, Bronx Community College alumna Claudia L. Edwards became executive director of the Reader's Digest Foundation. Like the foundation itself, Edwards is an advocate for children and literacy. She has worked for several service organizations, and she created the Tall Tree Initiative to unite libraries and public schools in an effort to better prepare children for the future.

United Way of America president and CEO Betty Stanley Beene, an alumna of Texarkana College, determines how her organization can best help people, especially children. Her wish is that every child grow up "with a strong sense of self-worth and promise for the future."

William Grace, who earned a degree at Berkshire Community College in Massachusetts, founded the Center for Ethical Leadership in Seattle. Through Grace's "4V" model of values, vision, voice, and virtue, the center promotes youth and community leadership.

Monroe Community College alumnus Foster N. Andersen holds one of the many awards he has received for his work in helping the disabled. In 1991, Andersen started Shared Adventures, whose mission is to bring "the outdoors into the lives of people with special needs and physical challenges."

CARTERET COMMUNITY COLLEGE

CATAWBA VALLEY COMMUNITY COLLEGE

CENTRAL CAROLINA COMMUNITY COLLEGE

CENTRAL PIEDMONT COMMUNITY COLLEGE

CLEVELAND COMMUNITY COLLEGE

COASTAL CAROLINA COMMUNITY COLLEGE

COLLEGE OF THE ALBEMARLE

CRAVEN COMMUNITY COLLEGE

DAVIDSON COUNTY COMMUNITY COLLEGE

DURHAM TECHNICAL COMMUNITY COLLEGE

EDGECOMBE COMMUNITY COLLEGE

FAYETTEVILLE TECHNICAL COMMUNITY COLLEGE

FORSYTH TECHNICAL COMMUNITY COLLEGE

GASTON COLLEGE

GUILFORD TECHNICAL COMMUNITY COLLEGE

HALIFAX COMMUNITY COLLEGE

HAYWOOD COMMUNITY COLLEGE

ISOTHERMAL COMMUNITY COLLEGE

JAMES SPRUNT COMMUNITY COLLEGE

JOHNSTON COMMUNITY COLLEGE

LENOIR COMMUNITY COLLEGE

LOUISBURG COLLEGE

MARTIN COMMUNITY COLLEGE

Leonard G. Butler, graduate of Arizona's Northland Pioneer College, spent more than 25 years as a law enforcement officer and served as chief of police for the Navajo Nation from 1994 to 2000. Butler encouraged his officers to continue their education by creating a classroom at one of the remote tribal police stations connected to Northland's interactive distance learning network.

Rio Hondo College's first police academy class in 1964 trained 28 graduates in six weeks. Today, classes of 75 train for 20 weeks. It is the largest community college-affiliated police academy in California, and many of its graduates go on to distinguished careers as police officers and chiefs.

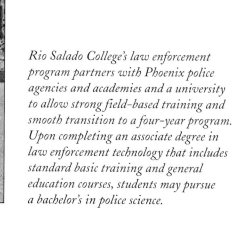

Rio Salado College's law enforcement program partners with Phoenix police agencies and academies and a university to allow strong field-based training and smooth transition to a four-year program. Upon completing an associate degree in law enforcement technology that includes standard basic training and general education courses, students may pursue a bachelor's in police science.

lege in 1984, Andersen studied engineering at the Rochester Institute of Technology. While there, he and a partner organized a program that made skiing accessible to people with special needs. In 1989, he moved to Santa Cruz, California. Discovering that the disabled community there had few recreational opportunities, he began Shared Adventures in 1991 to enable people with disabilities to enjoy the great outdoors.

Today, Shared Adventures offers year-round events and excursions, bringing the disabled and able-bodied communities together through kayaking, scuba diving, whale watching, indoor rock climbing, train excursions, hiking, camping, bird watching, and other activities. Andersen believes, "Anything can be accessible, with an accessible mind."

It was a different set of obstacles that faced former congressman Kweisi Mfume on the road to a life of public service. Born into a poor family, Mfume dropped out of high school at age 16. His mother had died and he needed a job. Though he worked hard, he also hung around the streets of West Baltimore with, as he later put it, "hoodlums, slickers, and wannabes." Then, one summer evening in 1972, he had a vision of his mother in which he saw both her unconditional love for him and her pain at what he had become. That night he turned his back on the streets and all they represented.

Mfume turned to education as the way to change the direction of his life. After working for his GED, he enrolled at Baltimore City Community College, did well, and subsequently earned a master's degree at Johns Hopkins University. In his 1996 autobiography, *No Free Ride*, he wrote, "I never ceased to wonder at how [education] freed me." During his student years, Mfume also became a campus and community activist, concerned with such problems as illiteracy, drugs, and low self-esteem. In 1979, he won a seat on the Baltimore City Council. Then in 1986, he was elected to Congress,

where he championed causes ranging from education and youth employment to expanding minority business opportunities and civil rights.

In 1995, the National Association for the Advancement of Colored People asked Mfume to head the troubled organization. Mfume accepted, knowing that "the NAACP would offer me the opportunity to fight for the rights of all people of color, free of partisan

Esther Moellering Tomljanovich, an Itasca Community College alumna, served as a Minnesota judge for 21 years, with eight of those as an associate justice on the state's supreme court. She also helped found Minnesota Women Lawyers, a nonprofit group "working to secure the full and equal participation of women in the legal profession and in a just society."

Ohio juvenile court judge Peter M. Sikora has initiated innovative programs that address issues such as child support, victim compensation, and community restitution through service projects. He serves on charitable and educational boards, including his alma mater's Cuyahoga Community College Foundation.

As governor of the Chickasaw Nation, **Bill Anoatubby** helped expand services in healthcare, housing, nutrition, education, job training, cultural preservation, and economic development. He also encouraged the Nation to provide scholarship funding to Oklahoma's Murray State College, his alma mater.

Jeane J. Kirkpatrick, alumna of Stephens College, Missouri, served on the National Security Council and was the first woman to serve as permanent representative to the United Nations. She received the Presidential Medal of Freedom, the nation's highest civilian award.

Maryland governor **Parris Glendening** takes the oath of office in 1999. First elected in 1994, the Broward Community College, Florida, graduate ran his campaign on the "five E's": education, enforcement, environment, economic growth, and excellence in government.

Miami-Dade Community College graduate Carol M. Browner values the "natural wonders of the United States." As EPA administrator, she worked for new safety standards and the speedy cleanup of hazardous waste sites.

Hawaii's first governor of Filipino ancestry, **Benjamin J. Cayetano**, a graduate of Los Angeles Harbor College, has received numerous public service honors, including the 1991 Exellence in Leadership Medallion for implementing a program to address the problem of latchkey children in the state's elementary schools.

Former U.S. Secretary of Labor Ray Marshall, alumnus of Mississippi's Hinds Community College, founded the Ray Marshall Center for the Study of Human Resources at the University of Texas to provide training and research on issues that affect workers' quality of life.

As the longest-serving governor of Minnesota, Hibbing Community College alumnus **Rudy Perpich**, who died in 1995, was an advocate for minorities, women, and people with disabilities.

*Representative **Ray LaHood** of Illinois, who attended Spoon River College and Illinois Central College, calls community college "the best educational buy there is." A former junior high school teacher, he was first elected to Congress in 1994.*

*Highline Community College alumnus **Norman B. Rice** served as mayor of Seattle from 1990 to 1997. As a city council member in 1983, Rice challenged the state legislature to make community and technical college funding as great a priority as funding for four-year institutions.*

*Henry B. **Gonzalez** of Texas, who attended San Antonio College, served in Congress for more than 35 years. He worked on legislation pertaining to veterans, education, economic development, civil rights, and safe drinking water.*

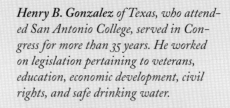

*At age 23, **J. Keith Arnold** became the youngest person ever elected to the Florida House of Representatives, where he served from 1982 to 1998. Of his alma mater, Edison Community College, he once said, "It is a place where dreams begin and never end."*

*Texas state representatives **Dawnna Dukes** (left) and **Terry Keel** (right) meet with fellow Austin Community College alumna **Judy Flakes Nwachie**, a professor at ACC and St. Edward's University. Dukes is an advocate for the working class and minorities, Keel serves on committees for public safety and criminal jurisprudence, and Nwachie has been honored for her human rights work.*

*In 1993, the U.S. Air Force honored Holmes Community College graduate **Samuel O. Massey** with the Excalibur Award, naming him the service's most outstanding surgeon. Before retiring in 1998, Massey worked as a medical missionary in Appalachia, Central America, and with Cuban refugees and others in need of medical help.*

*Community College of the Air Force, Alabama, alumnus **Eric W. Benken** served as chief master sergeant, the top noncommissioned officer advising on the welfare, effective utilization, and progress of enlisted soldiers. His decorations include the Distinguished Service Medal and the Legion of Merit.*

MILITARY

Douglas C. Verissimo, now assigned to the USS Stennis, flew with the elite U.S. Navy Flight Demonstration Squadron the Blue Angels from 1996 to 1999. He worked in his father's masonry contracting business before enrolling at Cape Cod Community College in Massachusetts, from which he graduated in 1987 with an associate degree in arts and science.

wrangling." It proved to be a good move for everyone. Mfume successfully eliminated the organization's $4 million debt and revitalized its image.

Awilda R. Marquez, a graduate of Maryland's Harford Community College, has served in a number of top-level positions, most recently as senior policy adviser to former U.S. Secretary of Commerce William M. Daley. Before joining the government, she helped found Women Entrepreneurs of Baltimore, a nonprofit organization that provides capital and training for women who wish to start their own businesses.

Marquez didn't begin her college career right away, choosing instead to travel and work abroad after high school graduation. Returning to the United States after more than a decade, she enrolled at HCC. "I still feel the thrill of their open-arm welcome of someone different," she says of her reception at the college. "I wasn't an 18-year-old coming in."

Harford officials nominated Marquez for a Harry S. Truman scholarship, established to promote public service careers among college students. The scholarship enabled her to attend Georgetown University, where she earned a bachelor of science degree in foreign service. After six years in the U.S. Foreign Service, she returned to obtain her law degree at the University of Maryland. "The [Truman] Foundation's vote of confidence changed my life," Marquez later said, "forging my commitment to public service forever."

Many community college alumni have also chosen to help others through federal, state, and city government service. Others have served in such critical areas as law enforcement, emergency rescue, and the military. Samuel Massey found a way to combine his surgical skills, his love of medical missionary work, and his commitment to his community college as a place of higher learning and as a place that prepares people to live in and contribute to their communities.

As a 21-year-old Air Force veteran, Massey enrolled at Holmes Community College in Mississippi. With the encouragement of a Holmes dean, who felt Massey was well suited to medicine, the young man studied math and science and went on to earn his medical degree at the University of Tennessee. He built a lucrative practice as a physician and surgeon and regularly donated 10 percent or more of his time to poor or low-income patients. In 1980, Massey began visiting Appalachia and eventually took his medical and surgical expertise to the poor in Haiti, Jamaica, Belize, and other countries. He donated $1 million to fund the Mobile Medical Mission Hospital, which provides medical and surgical support worldwide.

In 1990, Massey donated $500,000 to establish a scholarship fund for Holmes Community College healthcare students. Those who accept the full-tuition scholarship must agree to either donate 10 percent of their earnings after training to continue the fund or provide 10 percent of their working time free to those in need. "I realize I can't carry on the work I've been doing forever," Massey told the *Air Force News* in 1998. "My hope is for these students to continue where I eventually leave off."

The courage and willingness to serve that inspire many people to pursue military or law enforcement careers lead others to such demanding occupations as firefighting and emergency rescue. Hands-on experience is crucial for preparing students for these fields. Firefighting programs such as those at California's Crafton Hills College and Oregon's Portland Community College focus on practical exercises that create true-to-life situations. In addition to firefighting, students in these programs learn emergency medical rescue and hazardous material removal.

Students in the environmental technology program at California's Southwestern College learn how to handle hazardous waste. The college works with industry and government to train technicians in this vital area. Student Rosella Deguzman left her career in finance for this nontraditional field, which offers her "an opportunity to face exciting challenges."

Students in the Basic Fire Academy at California's Crafton Hills College get hands-on experience extinguishing a fire. Students also learn how to deal with hazardous materials and medical emergencies. To serve the community, explained 37-year veteran and academy supervisor Terry Koeper, a firefighter "must be a jack-of-all-trades."

Portland Community College fire science technology students learn vital skills at Oregon's Rocky Butte (below). The butte's challenging terrain is the perfect environment for students to practice tricky rescue operation procedures.

An Iowa rescue team uses the Jaws of Life to free a mock car crash victim during the 1998 International Extrication Competition. Illinois's Rock Valley College hosted the event as a community service and to raise the visibility of the firefighting profession.

The community served by the Mesa, Arizona, fire department benefits from a special collaboration between the department and Mesa Community College, one of the Maricopa Community Colleges. A team called the Connectors, made up of Mesa students, assists community members dealing with troubling, but nonemergency, situations. The Connectors link people with appropriate community services, which helps ensure that emergency personnel can remain on call.

Many two-year institutions provide students with experiences that help them gain civic awareness and with skills that let them contribute to their communities. Gulf Coast Community College in Florida has developed the Citizen Leadership Institute, which uses a curriculum of motivation and skill building to prepare a new generation of citizen leaders. Students attend training sessions and meet with civic leaders to discuss community issues. The college is "not just a meeting place, it's a catalyst," explains Pam Whitelock, GCCC's dean of lifelong learning.

Oakton Community College in Illinois intertwines a course in social psychology with an introduction in sociology to form The Civic Mind. The combined course has two instructors, but assignments and tests overlap. Students are required to complete 20 hours of service with a nonprofit agency or activity. Students consider what factors make up a civil society, and they

observe human behavior to discover what influences contribute to the health of a community and what influences contribute to the denigration of a community.

Los Angeles Southwest College found itself at the heart of civil turmoil in the wake of the 1991 Rodney King arrest, which took place less than a mile from the college. Citywide riots flared in protest to the beating of King by police officers. Neighborhoods where college students lived were destroyed. To head off further violence, the college community, faculty, and staff initiated a series of town hall meetings at the college. The meetings stabilized the community by providing a discussion forum open to everyone, including gang members, police officers, and elected officials.

Through such efforts, community colleges strive to build connections among community members and to dispel the stereotyping and fear that become associated with entire groups, including groups of people in uniform. Although colleges are rarely put to such an extreme test as that experienced by Los Angeles Southwest, the notion of institutional citizenship is one that resonates with community college leaders. Just as students are exhorted to act with integrity and show support for their communities, the colleges themselves must be responsibile for responding to community needs and for acting calmly in times of crisis.

Students (clockwise from front left) Boyce Turnbull, Jeff Cross, Kevin Stratman, and Mike Castillo joined the Connectors, a collaborative effort between Mesa Community College and the Mesa, Arizona, fire department. By assisting community members with nonemergency crises, the Connectors help ensure that fire department personnel are available to handle emergency calls.

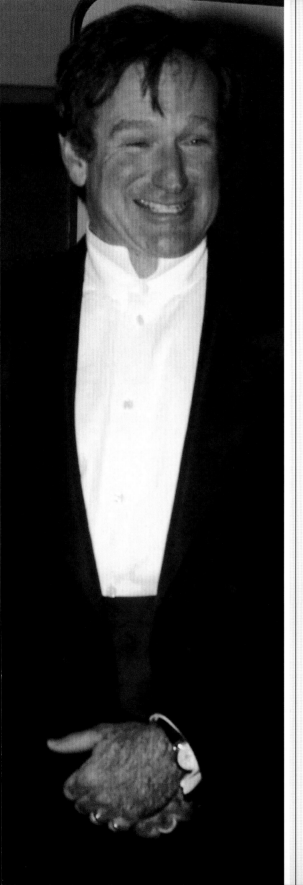

Taking the Stage

"THE COLLEGE OF DUPAGE WAS INSTRUMENTAL IN CHANGING MY LIFE AND GIVING ME DIRECTION."

—James Belushi, actor (College of DuPage, Illinois)

Dustin Hoffman took an acting class at Santa Monica College because a friend told him, "It's three credits and nobody flunks." Hoffman not only boosted his grade point average, he found his life's work. Theater teacher Mary Jean Sutcliff "just seemed to understand that a door was opened for me and that I was very passionate about it," he said at a 1999 press conference announcing his honorary chairmanship of a $25 million fundraising campaign for the college.

Hoffman, who has won two Academy Awards and has been nominated five other times, said that without Santa Monica College, "I'm quite sure I wouldn't have become an actor."

Community colleges have influenced other entertainers as well. Before he became an actor, Charles Dutton lived a street-tough adolescence in Baltimore that landed him in jail by age 16. For another conviction he went to the Maryland State Penitentiary, where his defiant attitude earned him a stint in solitary confinement. Dutton passed time reading an anthology of plays by black writers and emerged from solitary with the idea of forming a prison drama company.

Actor Robin Williams showed his versatility as a student at California's College of Marin, where his many roles in the early 1970s included Snoopy in You're a Good Man, Charlie Brown and Malvolio in Twelfth Night. Williams, who won an Oscar for his role in Good Will Hunting, has returned to Marin several times for comedy benefit performances, and he is a major contributor to the drama department's scholarship fund.

Students play Romeo and Juliet during Orange Coast College's 14th annual Shakespeare Month. The California college boasts three theaters on campus and a student-run repertory company. Film and stage actress Kelly McGillis attended Orange Coast, as did Academy Award–winning actress Diane Keaton, who toured overseas with fellow student actors in 1964, playing Maria in The Sound of Music.

Dutton told *The Washington Post* that acting opened his eyes to the power of the stage and its effect on an audience, motivating him to "discover my own humanity." Part of that discovery lay in earning a GED and an associate degree from Hagerstown Community College while in prison. After his release, Dutton studied drama at Yale and made it to Broadway, where he earned Tony Award nominations for his roles in *Ma Rainey's Black Bottom* and *The Piano Lesson*. He has appeared in movies including *Random Hearts* and *A Time to Kill*, and starred in the television series *Roc*.

Although Dutton's was a particularly dramatic entrance, many acclaimed actors and actresses approached their careers by way of a community college. For two-time Academy Award–winner Tom Hanks, whose movie credits include *Forrest Gump* and *Saving Private Ryan*, it was California's Chabot College. Marlee Matlin, who won an Academy Award in 1986 for her role in *Children of a Lesser God*, attended William Rainey Harper College in Illinois. Other stars who attended community colleges include Katharine Ross, Jane Curtin, Nick Nolte, Doug Sheehan, Elinor Donahue, and Sandy Duncan.

Annette Bening, twice nominated for a Best Actress Oscar and winner of a Tony Award, returned to San Diego Mesa College to give a speech and talk with drama students. Actress Lee Meriwether has also maintained ties to her alma mater. She generously contributed to the remodeling of the City College of San Francisco's Diego Rivera Theater and has returned to the college to work with students on stage productions.

Actor James Belushi says the College of DuPage "was instrumental in changing my life and giving me direction." He has raised hundreds of thousands of dollars for the college's

*A young **Sylvester Stallone** reads lines with fellow student actors for a 1967 play at Miami-Dade Community College. The actor is known for his starring role as prizefighter Rocky Balboa in the Rocky movie series and for such action-adventure films as Cliffhanger and Rambo.*

*Future film star **Annette Bening** rehearses a scene from The Pajama Game, a 1977 production at San Diego Mesa College. Bening majored in drama at the community college from 1976 to 1977, then transferred to San Francisco State University to complete her studies.*

Stephen Spinella *(right), shown in a scene from the Broadway production of Angels in America: Perestroika, won a Tony Award in 1994 for portraying the drama's AIDS-stricken hero. Spinella, who attended Arizona's Phoenix College, has also appeared in movies and on television.*

Actor-director **Morgan Freeman,** *who attended Los Angeles City College, has starred in such critically acclaimed dramas as Driving Miss Daisy, Glory, and The Shawshank Redemption. He has received three Academy Award nominations.*

At a news conference with President Piedad F. Robertson, **Dustin Hoffman** *announces a fundraising effort for Santa Monica College, which he attended for a year. The actor, who was awarded an honorary degree in 1989, holds a photo of himself as a member of the college's tennis team.*

Charles Dutton, *star of the television series Roc, has earned two Tony nominations and has appeared in several movies. The actor, who spent much of his youth in prison, earned an associate degree from Maryland's Hagerstown Community College and went on to study at Yale University's School of Drama.*

Television and film actress **Lee Meriwether,** *whose many roles included Catwoman in the 1966 Batman movie, began her acting career at City College of San Francisco as a radio and television/theater arts major. While there, she entered the Miss San Francisco pageant and went on to win the Miss America title in 1955.*

Actor and comedian **James Belushi,** *a 1974 graduate of the College of DuPage in Illinois, credits a DuPage professor with helping him stay in school and getting him involved with Chicago's Second City improv group, which he joined in 1977. Whenever Belushi returns to the campus, he takes time to meet with students.*

arts endowment. The John Belushi and Second City Theater Scholarship Fund he started in honor of his late brother, comedian John Belushi, who also attended DuPage, provides two full scholarships annually to theater students and three partial scholarships to music students. In 1999, James Belushi gave a benefit performance to inaugurate the John Belushi Artist-in-Residence Fund, which makes it possible for performance artists to spend extended periods of time on campus working with students.

Actor and director Bill Duke emulates the mentoring he received at New York's Dutchess Community College when he guides and instructs students at Howard University, where he is co-chair of the radio, television, and film department. The 1963 graduate has appeared in films including *Predator, American Gigolo,* and *Menace II Society;* directed *A Rage in Harlem* and *Deep Cover;* and won an Emmy for producing *A Raisin in the Sun* on television. Duke credits his Dutchess professors with sparking his interest in the arts and says the college's first president, James Hall, helped him achieve his educational goals. Duke relates that Hall even assisted him with tuition when he learned that Duke was planning to drop out of Boston University because of financial difficulties. "That was the start of me thinking of myself and the world in a very different way," Duke said.

The crew on this film shoot at Disney/MGM Studios is composed of students from Valencia Community College in Florida. The college offers a two-year degree for fields such as production management, camera operations, lighting, editing, sound, and set construction. Valencia counts among its graduates filmmaker Gregg Hale, producer of the 1999 low-budget horror flick Blair Witch Project.

5 Liberal & Fine Arts

"I SAY ALL OF YOU IN THIS ROOM ARE REALLY POETS. YOU'RE JUST LIKE ME, CHURNING INSIDE ALL THE TIME. YOU HAVE YOUR DELIGHTS AND YOUR AGONIES."
—*Gwendolyn Brooks, Pulitzer Prize-winning poet (Kennedy-King College, Illinois)*

Mexican muralist Diego Rivera, a compassionate advocate of the common people, believed that art belonged on the walls of public buildings, not in museums—a conviction appreciated by instructor Tina Martin and her students at the City College of San Francisco. Martin, who teaches English as a second language, uses Rivera's mural *Pan American Unity (left)* to expose her international students to art from the Americas and to help them learn English.

Rivera's mural, acquired by the college at the beginning of World War II, depicts various North and South American figures, from ancient gods to modern-day inventors, laborers, and artisans. Under Martin's tutelage, students first focus on Rivera's artistic techniques and humanitarian vision, then they research sections of the painting and complete writing assignments. Through this combination of activities they polish their language skills, sharpen their critical-thinking abilities, and enhance their cultural understanding.

The passion and compassion that infused Rivera's works, and inspire Martin and her students, underlie the work of many people who make the arts and hu-

*Photographer **John H. White**, who graduated from Central Piedmont Community College in North Carolina, received a Pulitzer Prize in 1982 for his work at the Chicago Sun-Times. White, who says he "captures life from birth to death, especially the things in between," has photographed such widely divergent subjects as South African president Nelson Mandela and a museum worker struggling to brush the teeth of a dinosaur specimen.*

89

Sam Grant, a Miami-Dade Community College professor, advises his graphic arts students during a class discussion of collage and typography. Students select from two associate degree programs in graphic design to prepare them for careers in advertising and publishing.

An Ohlone College student takes advantage of the school's idyllic setting in Fremont, California, to fulfill requirements for an art class. Overlooking San Francisco Bay, the college was named in 1967 to honor the Ohlone Indians of the Costanoan tribe, who once inhabited the area.

Wes Towne, a 95-year-old Salinas, California, resident, works at the potter's wheel in a ceramics class at Hartnell College. Aspiring artists of all ages and cultural backgrounds participate in community college arts programs for professional and personal achievement.

manities their career. Community colleges provide a foundation of skills from which a variety of talents can grow: In the 1996-97 academic year, nearly 170,000 associate degrees in liberal arts were awarded to community college students.

Encouraging students to explore their creativity and show the results to the world is the responsibility of art instructors like Gregory Kondos, now retired from the faculty of Sacramento City College in California. After serving in the Navy during World War II, Kondos enrolled in art classes at SCC. Excited by his early success in the classroom, he took every art class the college offered. "I kept forgetting you could graduate," he quipped. Finally, he did leave SCC to complete his studies at the University of California, Davis. But he wasn't gone for good. Kondos returned to fill a faculty post at SCC that he held until his retirement in 1982. From 1956, he managed the campus art gallery, staging monthly exhibits of students' work and showing the work of outstanding artists from the region.

With their talent and the help of nurturing instructors, many alumni have built impressive careers. Dancer Bella Lewitzky, who attended San Bernardino Valley College in California, toured the globe for 30 years with the dance company she founded. Rock musician Tom Petty got his start at St. Petersburg Junior College in Florida in the 1960s. Composer and musician Mark Mancina, who attended California's Golden West College, went on to score dozens of commercials and films, including *The Lion King*.

Among Hollywood insiders, Ron Jones is known for turning out popular soundtracks for film and television, including the music for *Star Trek: The Next Generation*. But to faculty and students at Clackamas Community College in Oregon, Jones is better known for catapulting the music department into the computer

Rachel Chen, a ceramics student at Collin County Community College District in Texas, displays some of her work. Chen had no experience with pottery before taking classes in 1994, but she quickly mastered the craft, perfecting a firing technique that produces a mottled finish.

VISUAL ARTISTS

Kit Carson, a 1980 graduate of Yavapai College in Arizona, shapes whimsical metal sculptures, as well as glass items and jewelry, in his studio in New River, Arizona. Carson has presented his alma mater with several of his works, which have been installed in the college's courtyard.

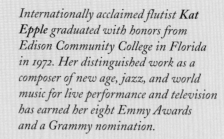

Internationally acclaimed flutist **Kat Epple** graduated with honors from Edison Community College in Florida in 1972. Her distinguished work as a composer of new age, jazz, and world music for live performance and television has earned her eight Emmy Awards and a Grammy nomination.

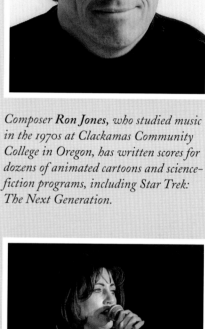

Since his 1963 graduation from Florida's St. Petersburg Junior College, pianist and composer **Stephen Montague** has played on stages in Paris and London and at New York's Carnegie Hall. His compositions are frequently performed by the London Symphony Orchestra and have drawn audiences in the thousands to the John F. Kennedy Center for the Performing Arts in Washington, D.C.

Pianist **Jon Nakamatsu** earned an associate degree at California's Foothill College and bachelor's and master's degrees in German studies from Stanford before pursuing music full time. In 1997, at age 28, he won the prestigious Van Cliburn International Piano Competition—the first American to win in 16 years.

Composer **Ron Jones**, who studied music in the 1970s at Clackamas Community College in Oregon, has written scores for dozens of animated cartoons and science-fiction programs, including Star Trek: The Next Generation.

MUSICIANS

From left, Randy Owen, Jeff Cook, Teddy Gentry, and Mark Herndon make up the country music super-group Alabama. **Randy Owen** graduated from Northeast Alabama Community College in 1971, and his cousin **Jeff Cook** attended Alabama's Gadsden State Community College. Owen and Cook have shown appreciation to their alma maters through generous fundraising efforts.

Country music star **Lee Ann Womack** studied music at South Plains College in Texas, one of the first colleges to offer a degree in bluegrass and country music. The singer, who signed with Decca Records in 1996, toured with her college's band, The Country Caravan.

age. Despite a full workload that includes an online music school with students from 17 countries, Jones, who was a student at Clackamas in the 1970s, returns to lead seminars for students enrolled in the college's highly regarded music program. As one colleague expressed it, Jones has brought the school into the 21st century. "Fully half of the classes now offered at CCC are available only because of his influence," said faculty member Gary Nelson.

Randy Owen, rhythm guitarist and lead singer of the country music group Alabama, graduated in 1971 from Northeast Alabama Community College. The group has won more than 150 major music awards, including the Academy of Country Music's Artist of the Decade honor for the 1980s. For nearly 20 years, the group sponsored the annual June Jam fishing tournament and country music festival in Fort Payne, Ala-bama, which drew more than 60,000 fans and benefited several local causes, including Owen's alma mater. He says he was able to stay in college and earn his associate degree in part because of Northeast's low tuition. To help extend to others the opportunity for a college education, Owen established a scholarship fund at Northeast. Owen's cousin Jeff Cook, also a member of Alabama, attended Gadsden State Community College and has also helped his college, raising nearly $1 million for its endowment fund.

Students and local musicians assemble at Cottey College in Missouri for a musicale in the early 1900s. Founded in 1884 by Virginia Alice Cottey as a two-year liberal arts college for women, the school first distinguished itself in the field of music and has since graduated more than 10,000 women in the arts and sciences.

Many community college alumni extend themselves in order to give back to their alma maters, and the institutions themselves often assume responsibility for giving their communities an opportunity for continuing cultural enrichment. In many areas, a community college may represent its community's only center for the arts. In other cases the colleges supplement existing public and private programs. Universally, arts programming sponsored by community colleges addresses local needs and broadens local perspectives.

Cuyahoga Community College launched its Tri-C JazzFest Cleveland in 1980, and what began as a modest two-day affair has since grown to 10 days and has drawn such jazz legends as Ella Fitzgerald, Tony Bennett, Dizzy Gillespie, Miles Davis, and Herbie Hancock. On the college's three campuses and at venues around town, jazz greats and other invited guests perform each spring to sold-out halls, while back in the classroom, aspiring jazz musicians gather for individualized instruction.

JazzFest clinics and workshops address everything from improvisation to stage fright. Area elementary and high school students are encouraged to attend concerts designed especially for them, and to participate in competitions judged by the festival's visiting musicians. Students also enjoy "informances," listening to live performances and learning about the musical roots and techniques of the jazz art form.

The popular Miami Book Fair International, now in its second decade, takes place at Miami-Dade Com-

Every spring, Cuyahoga Community College's Tri-C JazzFest Cleveland draws big-name artists to Ohio. They perform for students on the school's three campuses and at concert halls and theaters around the city. Cuyahoga sponsors a number of jazz programs that together reach 40,000 people per year.

The Northland Community Band, cosponsored by Northland Community and Technical College and the city of Thief River Falls, Minnesota, represented the United States in its division at the Ninth International Music Festival in Sydney, Australia, in 1998. The band includes community members as well as students from the college and from area high schools.

Music student Eric Chambers practices and composes in the college's state-of-the-art MIDI (musical instrument digital interface) lab at Johnson County Community College, Kansas.

Two student actors at Minnesota's North Hennepin Community College apply makeup in a backstage dressing room. Theater courses at the college include the foundations of acting—such as movement, improvisation, and character development—as well as design and technical studies.

Fashion and costume design student Lisa Marquese inspects her handiwork before a production of Romeo and Juliet at Orange Coast College in California. Besides a program for aspiring actors, the college offers an entertainment technology program that prepares students for theater careers in lighting, sound, set design, and costuming.

munity College's Wolfson campus in Florida. The fair features miles of bookstalls, a full-scale children's program, and appearances by best-selling authors, playwrights, and poets.

Although community college liberal arts majors do not necessarily seek fame, community colleges can sometimes provide opportunities for students to gain local and national recognition. Sharon Greytak, an independent filmmaker and 1978 graduate of Housatonic Community College in Connecticut, has 10 films to her credit. Her *Weirded Out and Blown Away*, which chronicles the lives of young disabled people just beginning their careers, won wide viewership when it was

aired on public television stations across the country. Like Greytak, who uses a wheelchair, the film's subjects have all triumphed over adversity, never losing sight of their goals. To Greytak, Housatonic is a place to build "strong confidence," where "new ideas about the world are tested and refined through the understanding of the lives of others."

Other community college students with a passion for film have distinguished themselves and brought recognition to the colleges that gave them their start. In 1999, more than 750 colleges and universities were invited to apply to the second annual National Student Festival for Film, Video, and New Media held at New York's Hunter College. Only 35 submissions were ac-

Robert Moses, founder and artistic director of the Robert Moses Kin dance company, uses physicality, fluid movement, and music to make social commentary. Moses, who joined the dance faculty at Stanford University in 1994, began his dance training at Orange Coast College in California. "The training and view of art in the world I received at Orange Coast," he says, "were the finest I could have found anywhere."

Novelist and poet **Rita Mae Brown** attended Florida's Broward Community College in the 1960s before publishing *Rubyfruit Jungle*, the 1973 novel that scandalized critics and readers with its bawdy tales of heroine Molly Bolt. Now viewed as an American classic, it has sold more than a million copies. She has also written mystery novels "cowritten" by Brown's cat Sneaky Pie.

Before turning to theater, playwright and actor **Sam Shepard** studied agriculture at California's Mt. San Antonio Community College in 1960. Shepard has appeared in films including *The Right Stuff* and *Snow Falling on Cedars*, but his plays, notably the Pulitzer Prize–winning *Buried Child*, are his most lasting contribution to American culture.

Winner of a 1950 Pulitzer Prize—the first African American poet so honored—**Gwendolyn Brooks** attended Chicago's Wilson Junior College (now Kennedy-King College) in the 1930s. Her chronicles of the African American experience won her international recognition, including an appointment as consultant in poetry to the Library of Congress and membership in the prestigious Society for Literature at the University of Thessaloniki in Greece.

Award-winning screenwriter **John Fusco**, who attended Naugatuck Valley Community College in Connecticut, wrote the box office smash *Young Guns* and its sequel, *Young Guns II*. His first screenplay was for the 1986 movie *Crossroads*, a classic among blues fans.

Civil War scholar and historian **David Herbert Donald** began his academic career in the 1930s at Holmes Community College in Mississippi. Now a Harvard University professor emeritus, Donald has written and edited dozens of books and has won two Pulitzer Prizes.

A 1978 graduate of Mountain Empire Community College in Virginia, **Rita Sims Quillen** celebrates Appalachian life in three collections of poetry. As a faculty member at Northeast State Technical Community College in Tennessee, Quillen is on the other side of the desk, encouraging students in the writer's craft.

cepted. Among the entrants were Pittaya "Pete" Tun-siricharolengul and Brian Sanchez, student videographers at San Antonio College, Texas. The pair's four-minute video, *Time and Fate*, a dream sequence in which a mother drops her child at school, placed in the semifinals along with entries from major universities. Besides bringing them national attention, the experience infused the students with even more enthusiasm for their studies and their careers. "This is a case of two outstanding students raising each other up," observed San Antonio College professor Fred Weiss.

A word of encouragement has made the difference in many a person's life. Gwendolyn Brooks, a 1936 graduate of Wilson Junior College in Chicago (now Kennedy-King College), began writing poetry at age seven, inspired by her father, a master storyteller. When she was 16, a chance meeting with legendary poet Langston Hughes, who praised her work, inspired Brooks to keep writing. "I lived on those words, ohhh, for a long time," she told *The Houston Chronicle*.

Brooks, who died in December 2000, won the Pulitzer Prize in 1950 for her work *Annie Allen*. She was awarded the prestigious Senior Fellowship in Literature from the National Endowment for the

In the 1920s, the Hillsboro Junior College library afforded a place for quiet study. At what is now Hill College in Texas, the library still serves as a center for student research and includes a special collection of Civil War history.

Humanities, was a consultant in poetry to the Library of Congress, and had served as the poet laureate of Illinois since 1968. She kept up a rigorous schedule of readings, traveling to approximately 50 schools and campuses, hospitals, and prisons each year to address and encourage her audiences.

Noted Civil War historian David Herbert Donald, whose book *Charles Sumner and the Coming of the Civil War* earned him a Pulitzer Prize in 1961, credits a community college for his start. Known especially for his studies of Abraham Lincoln and other Civil War figures, Donald built on his early education at Holmes Community College in Mississippi, going on to earn his doctorate from the University of Illinois. He then distinguished himself as a professor of history at Johns Hopkins, Princeton, Columbia, and Harvard universities, and at Smith College. Donald was awarded a second Pulitzer in 1988 for the biography *Look Homeward: A Life of Thomas Wolfe.*

Community college alumni have made valuable contributions to every academic and career field. For some, the experience inspired them to dedicate their career to community colleges. Graduates return to teach or serve as institution presidents. Others have established community college leadership programs at universities. Through their valued writing, teaching, and leadership, community college alumni have championed and challenged the community college mission.

TransPacific Hawaii College student Yuko Jinno, who is Japanese, practices her English skills while visiting with Joan Cholar at the Unity Church in Honolulu. TransPacific's associate in arts degree is preceded by six months of intensive ESL study, and community outreach is part of the ESL curriculum. The college enrolls students from throughout Asia.

Tulsa Community College student and Phi Theta Kappa 1999–2000 international president Stephanie Wright gathers with local children in Oklahoma, helping to carry out one of the honor society's missions, promoting literacy. Says Wright, "It's important to promote the role students play to foster literacy."

Students often choose community colleges because of their convenient location, open access, and reasonable cost. They use their general education credits either toward an associate degree or to transfer to a bachelor's degree program through the growing partnerships between two-year and four-year institutions.

To accomplish their goals, students must have not only access to higher education but encouragement from mentors. That's the goal of Ellen Olmstead, an English professor at Bristol Community College in Massachusetts. On the faculty since 1994, Olmstead was named outstanding community college professor of 1999 by the Carnegie Foundation and *USA Today*. Referred to as a "powerhouse" and a "guardian angel" by her students, Olmstead has taken on private counseling and tutoring in addition to her teaching load. Most recently, she has worked with Head Start to College, an outreach program serving usually older, "truly nontraditional" students who come to a rented church space for classes, seminars, drop-in tutoring, and social time. To explain her commitment, Olmstead quotes Marian Wright Edelman, founder and director of the Children's Defense Fund: "Service is the very fabric of our lives—the rent we pay for living on the planet."

Extending herself and her writing and literature classes to students who often have given up on themselves, Olmstead is mindful of the diverse ethnic backgrounds of the student body. She includes works by Puerto Rican, African American, and Native American authors in her literature courses, bearing out an enduring and central truth of literature: It has the power to embrace all people and to serve as a reflection of our common humanity.

Rod Risley, an alumnus of San Jacinto College in Texas, is executive director of Phi Theta Kappa, the largest honor society in American higher education. Established in 1918, the society recognizes and encourages scholarship among community college students. To wear the Phi Theta Kappa pin, shown below, students must complete a minimum of 12 hours of degree course work and maintain a 3.5 grade point average.

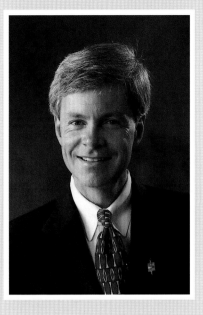

EDUCATION

*At age 21, U.S. Marine veteran **David R. Pierce** entered Fullerton College, California, calling it his "last, best chance." A teacher there encouraged him, and he went on to earn a Ph.D. in mathematics education. Inspired by his own experience, Pierce made a career of serving community colleges as professor, college president, and chancellor, and as president of the American Association of Community Colleges, from which he retired in 2000. Esteemed for his leadership and enduring commitment, Pierce believes "the fundamental issue is access. This is the principle on which community colleges were founded, and it is the tenet in which those who strive to advance the purposes and progress of the nation's community colleges believe with every fiber of their beings."*

Into the Future

"If you make the most of your community college experience, it will take you wherever you want to go."

—*Heidi White, International President, Phi Theta Kappa (Burlington County College, New Jersey)*

Community colleges began as a practical solution to the problem of adults needing affordable postsecondary education close to home. No one predicted that in less than a century they would become the largest, and arguably the most dynamic, sector of higher education in the United States.

Community colleges have been called the key to the American dream—"dream catchers," as Jerry Sue Thornton described them in her inauguration as president of Ohio's Cuyahoga Community College. To management expert Tom Peters, community colleges are "the unsung, underfunded backbone of America's all-important lifelong learning network." They have become one of the primary drivers of the national economy as well as partners in students' efforts for personal empowerment. Courses, programs, and partnerships are woven into the fabric of communities across the nation, where each college strives to reflect its community. Benefiting from this cooperation are technology students like Jim Uomoto at Pima Community College, Arizona *(left)*, who learns to etch wafers for microchips using a machine donated by Intel Corporation.

Janine Pease Pretty-on-Top, Little Big Horn College president for two decades, stands with Crow elders Barney Old Coyote and Joseph Medicine Crow at the Montana college's 1996 commencement. Tribal leaders' participation exemplifies the blending of contemporary education and native culture offered at tribal colleges.

Under the leadership of President Antonio Pérez, Borough of Manhattan Community College became a partner in the TeleMedia Accelerator, a public-private venture that helps small high-tech businesses grow, similar to traditional business incubators but with an emphasis on more advanced companies. The college provides advantageous office space near New York's "Silicon Alley" in exchange for an equity share in the venture.

As community colleges look to the future, they possess a tremendous asset they did not have a century ago: a rich history of success. A unifying force in that success are national leadership groups such as the American Association of Community Colleges, founded in 1920 and led in recent years by George R. Boggs, David R. Pierce, Dale Parnell, and Edmund J. Gleazer Jr.

Boggs believes the colleges owe their success to four enduring values: access, community responsiveness, creativity, and a focus on student learning. "Community college faculty and staff have been among the most creative and innovative of leaders in the effort to improve teaching and services." Yet, he says, "we cannot take our success for granted. The leaders of the future will need to be strong advocates of the core values of community colleges and must be willing to take the risks needed to maintain their viability in a new world."

That world will belong to the students of today—students like Yolanda Sanchez at Arizona's South Mountain Community College. Sanchez took advantage of Bridges to a Baccalaureate, a program that encourages minority students to pursue science, and as a result she decided to take a third year at her community college to accommodate her new major, life science with a focus on genetics. Sanchez plans to pursue a career in public policy, so she can help influence Congress on issues surrounding genetic science. Remarkably, although Sanchez grew up in an affluent neighborhood, she purposefully chose a community college noted for its poverty and diversity. "I grew up in an all-white neighborhood," says Sanchez, "but I'm Latina and Mexican American myself, so I chose a little college in south Phoenix that's 60 percent Hispanic and 75 percent minority." Her learning experience has gone far beyond academic course work. She has learned about herself and about life.

Sanchez observed her college's broad influence on the surrounding community, from the outreach center welcoming kids, to an after-school program that encourages interaction between elementary and college students. Hundreds of miles away, Sanchez gained first-hand knowledge of the growing "global village." During a five-week program that she describes as the "highlight of her college experience," she lived with a family in Guanajuato, Mexico, experiencing their language, culture, and values.

Technology not only enhances field training but broadens course delivery options. Students in Sweadner Hall at Frederick Community College, Maryland (left), view large dual-projection screens and interact with instructors using microphones and voting pads at each seat. Satellite dishes like those at Dallas County Community College District (background) allow colleges to send and receive courses worldwide.

A focus on the international has also culminated Heidi White's community college experience. Currently serving as international president for Phi Theta Kappa honor society, White avoided college after high school, choosing instead to go immediately into a job in sales. But at age 30, she lost her job and found herself at a crossroads, at which point, she says, "I didn't feel I had a lot of options."

Like many adults returning to the classroom after some years, White was apprehensive about her prospects for success. Because it seemed less intimidating than a four-year institution, she chose nearby Burlington County College, New Jersey, and began to thrive.

Her confidence grew as she brought home As. It was then she realized "I could handle college-level work."

White has been accepted to the University of Pennsylvania to continue her studies and intends to work in business and marketing. "At one point, I didn't have options. Now the doors of opportunity are opening up all around me," she says. When she meets people who face the kinds of challenges she did four years ago, she says, "I encourage people to come to community college with an open mind and seek out the opportunities, because they are endless. If you make the most of your community college experience, it will take you wherever you want to go."

Despite a difficult home life that made her feel she had "little hope left," Erika Cuevas vowed "I won't give up the dream of becoming a teacher and giving my heart to my students as well as any person in need." She graduated from Colorado Mountain College as an Alpine Bank Hispanic scholar, a program inspired by Alpine Bank CEO J. Robert Young. She then transferred to the University of Northern Colorado with plans to become an elementary school teacher. Cuevas is the first person in her family to earn a college degree.

1920...The American Association of Junior Colleges...became a forum for community college issues and a source of mutual support for its members at a time when the potential of the junior college was not widely understood or appreciated.

1862 **Passage of the Morrill Act**
With its emphasis on agriculture and on the mechanical arts, the Morrill Act of 1862, often referred to as the Land Grant Act, expanded access to public higher education, introduced the teaching of new types of courses, and included types of students previously excluded from higher education.

1870 **The Kalamazoo Decision**
The Michigan Supreme Court ruled that local school districts could construct and operate comprehensive high schools from public school funds. This precedent-setting decision opened the way for the development of the modern, comprehensive high school, which would, by the beginning of the 20th century, provide many public community colleges with their initial home.

1901 **Founding of Joliet Junior College, Illinois**
One of the earliest beneficiaries of the construction of large, modern high schools was Joliet Junior College. Founded under the influence of William Rainey Harper, president of the University of Chicago, Joliet Junior College is the oldest continuously existing public two-year college in the nation. While the junior college's courses were initially mixed in with those of the Joliet high school, by 1915 the junior college's enrollment had grown to such an extent that it added a "junior college wing." This was the nation's first major facility constructed specifically for use by a public junior college.

1904 **The Wisconsin Idea**
The University of Wisconsin emphasized that its mission was to assist the general public through extension services and to provide support to the state government. The university declared that the entire state was its campus. Today, most community colleges view individual service regions as their campuses.

1917 **Adoption of Junior College Accreditation Standards**
The North Central Association of Schools and Colleges established specific standards for the accreditation of public and private junior colleges. These standards, governing such areas as admissions policies, faculty qualifications, and minimum funding levels, not only brought a degree of uniformity to the young junior college movement but also demonstrated the willingness of and capacity for junior colleges to participate in America's unique system of institutional self-regulation.

1918 **Founding of Phi Theta Kappa Honor Society**
Phi Theta Kappa was founded to recognize and encourage academic achievement by two-year

college students and to provide them with opportunities for individual growth and development in academics, leadership, and service.

1920 **Founding of the American Association of Junior Colleges**
Called together by Philander Claxton, U.S. commissioner of education, and his higher education specialist, George Zook, more than 25 public and private junior college leaders met in St. Louis to organize the American Association of Junior Colleges. The association, proposed by the U.S. Bureau of Education to function as an accrediting body for the rapidly growing number of junior colleges, became a forum for community college issues and a source of mutual support for its members at a time when the potential of the junior college was not widely understood or appreciated.

1921 **California Legislation Fostering Independent Community College Districts**
Using proceeds from the federal Oil and Mineral Act, the California legislature created a Junior College Fund, the nation's first, to support the operation of locally governed junior college districts operating independently of the public high schools. California's Junior College Act of 1921 came to serve as a model for other states as they sought to put junior colleges on a sound fiscal and policy footing.

1928 **The First State Junior College Board**
Mississippi was the first state in the nation to organize a statewide governing board with specific oversight responsibility for the public junior colleges within its boundaries. The state's governing board worked closely with elected local boards in developing a strong network of public junior colleges that effectively balanced transfer and vocational programs.

1930 **The Asheville Decision**
Even as late as 1930, many state legislatures had yet to adopt specific legislation permitting communities to organize public junior colleges. This legal oversight did not deter communities, which organized junior colleges without explicit legal authority, much as they had organized high schools in the preceding century. The right of a community to take such a step was challenged in Asheville, North Carolina, with the North Carolina Supreme Court eventually ruling in favor of the community and its right to meet the educational needs of its citizens as it saw fit. This decision did much to secure the legal standing of those public junior colleges that were still being operated without the benefit of state legislation.

1944 **Passage of GI Bill of Rights**
U.S. Congress passed the Servicemen's Readjustment Act, popularly known as the GI Bill, to provide financial assistance for veterans of World War II who wished to pursue higher education. Building on smaller federal student aid programs developed at the end of the Great Depression, the GI Bill represented the federal government's first attempt to provide student aid on a large scale, helping to break down the economic and social barriers to attending college.

1947 *Higher Education for American Democracy*
Published by the President's Commission on Higher Education, this report, popularly known as the Truman Commission report, called for several things, including the expansion of a network of public community colleges that would charge little or no tuition; serve as cultural centers; be comprehensive in their program offerings with an emphasis on civic responsibilities; and serve the area in which they were located. The commission helped popularize the term *community college.*

1958 **Introduction of ADN Programs**
With funding support from the W. K. Kellogg Foundation and Rockefeller family, community colleges in New York, California, Florida, and other states introduced two-year programs leading to an associate degree in nursing (ADN) that entitled degree holders to sit for licensure as professional nurses.

1960 **W. K. Kellogg Foundation Support of Community College Leadership Development**
The W. K. Kellogg Foundation announced a series of grants to be used to establish university centers preparing a new generation of two-year college leaders. In all, 12 universities established junior college leadership programs. Hundreds of future deans and presidents would eventually graduate from the Kellogg Junior College Leadership Programs.

1960 **California Master Plan for Higher Education**
The three segments of California public higher education—the community colleges, comprehensive colleges and universities, and the University of California—agreed to a voluntary plan to divide responsibility for the state's rapidly growing number of undergraduates and provide the state's residents with the broadest possible range of educational opportunity without wasteful competition among the sectors.

1963– **Federal Aid to Higher Education**
1965 With the adoption of the Higher Education Facilities Act of 1963 and the first Higher Education Act of 1965, the federal government dramatically expanded its direct aid to community colleges and their students. Through the Facilities Act of 1963, communities were given the means to construct new campuses and enlarge existing facilities. Through the Higher Education Act of 1965, and its subsequent reauthorizations, the federal government provided a range of direct grants and loans to students based on need as a means of lessening the barrier of cost to higher education access.

1968 **Creation of the League for Innovation in the Community College**
The League for Innovation in the Community College is a consortium committed to improving community colleges through innovation, experimentation, and institutional transformation.

1970 **Open Admissions at City University of New York**
Breaking with a long-established tradition of selective admissions, the City University of New York ended its policy of granting admission to only the most academically gifted graduates of New York's public high schools, and guaranteed admission to all high school graduates. This policy change led to a rapid increase in enrollment, the introduction of large-scale developmental programs, and the organization of innovative community colleges in communities with the greatest economic need.

1971– **Federal Aid for Strengthening**
1978 **Tribal Colleges**
Beginning with Navajo Community College (now Diné College, Arizona) in 1971, AACC assisted in winning federal aid for the construction and maintenance of community colleges operating under the jurisdiction of Native American tribes. These efforts culminated in 1978 with the adoption of the Tribally Controlled Community College Assistance Act and the expansion of the community college to previously underserved communities throughout the West.

1972 **Name Change for Association**
The American Association of Junior Colleges changed its name to the American Association of Community and Junior Colleges in 1972 to reflect the broadening terminology used by the institutions.

1972 **Establishment of Association of Community College Trustees (ACCT)**
ACCT represents more than 6,500 elected and appointed trustees who govern more than 1,200 community, technical, and junior colleges in the United States, Canada, and England. ACCT offers trustee training and professional development programs, educational programs, research and publications, extensive board services, and public policy advocacy.

1978 Proposition 13 in California

The passage of Proposition 13 in California signaled the beginning of an increased demand by the public for greater accountability from its public institutions. Community colleges were in the forefront in adopting strategies for ensuring the most effective use of public funds in an era of fiscal constraint.

1988 Commission on the Future of Community Colleges Report

The commission's report, *Building Communities: A Vision for a New Century,* defined *community* "not only as a region to be served, but also as a climate to be created." Community colleges were challenged to assume a leadership role in creating a renewed climate of community in their service regions.

1992 Second Name Change for Association

The association changed its name to the American Association of Community Colleges in an effort to unify its diverse membership of technical, junior, and community colleges.

1998 Hope Scholarship and Lifetime Learning Tax Credits Established

The Hope "scholarship" is a tax credit available to eligible students during their first two years of postsecondary education. The tax credit is available for two tax years to those students who have not completed the first two years of postsecondary education. The Lifetime Learning credit is available for education beyond the first two years of college.

1998 Workforce Investment Act

This law substantially alters the federal government's role in job training, adult education, and vocational rehabilitation. Community colleges will still have a major role in the delivery of training services, but there will be a new order in the system. Training will be delivered primarily through Individual Training Accounts (or vouchers) and one-stop career center systems.

1998 Carl D. Perkins Vocational-Technical Education Act Reauthorization

The Perkins Act represents the major federal commitment to vocational education activities. The reauthorization removes set-asides historically included in the law for special populations and provides states flexibility in determining how best to spend Perkins dollars. Community colleges are considered important providers of postsecondary vocational education.

2000 New Expeditions Report

The W. K. Kellogg-funded New Expeditions project aimed to set a vision and strategic direction for the nation's community colleges for the first part of the 21st century. Relying on input from the field and critical analysis of trends, the project culminated in *The Knowledge Net: Connecting Communities, Learners, and Colleges,* which challenged community colleges through a series of recommendations for action.

2001 Community College Centennial

As the community college turns 100, it continues to evolve, responding to the needs of society at large while retaining its core commitment to equal access.

FEDERATED STATES OF MICRONESIA

COMMUNITY COLLEGE OF MICRONESIA—FSM

GUAM

GUAM COMMUNITY COLLEGE

NORTHERN MARIANAS ISLANDS

NORTHERN MARIANAS COLLEGE

PALAU

PALAU COMMUNITY COLLEGE

PUERTO RICO

COLEGIO UNIVERSITARIO DEL ESTE

INSTITUTO COMERCIAL DE PUERTO RICO JUNIOR COLLEGE

INTERAMERICAN UNIVERSITY OF PUERTO RICO *Two-Year Branch Campuses*

PONTIFICIA UNIVERSIDAD CATOLIC DE PUERTO RICO

PONTIFICIA UNIVERSIDAD CATOLIC DE PUERTO RICO
—ARECIBO
—GUAYAMA
—MAYAGUEZ

RAMIREZ COLLEGE OF BUSINESS TECHNOLOGY

UNIVERSITY OF PUERTO RICO AT AGUADILLA

UNIVERSITY OF PUERTO RICO
—CAROLINA REGIONAL COLLEGE
—LA MONTANA REGIONAL COLLEGE

Distinguished Community College Alumni

The following list includes distinguished community college alumni identified as of fall 2000. They appear according to AACC Outstanding Alumni Award categories. A * symbol indicates winners of the award. A + symbol indicates nominees. The college's current name appears here.

BUSINESS, INDUSTRY, AND MEDIA

FRED ADAMS
  East Mississippi Community College, Mississippi

WYLIE A. AITKEN +
  Santa Ana College, California

ELMER L. ANDERSEN +
  Minnesota State College—Southeast Technical, Minnesota

BRADBURY ANDERSON
  Waldorf College, Iowa

ELMER L. ANDERSON *
  Muskegon Community College, Michigan

WALTER ANDERSON +
  Westchester Community College, New York

KEITH MARLIN ANSPACH +
  Motlow State Community College, Tennessee

NOLAN D. ARCHIBALD *
  Dixie State College of Utah, Utah

JHANE BARNES
  Fashion Institute of Technology, New York

LINDA BEAUCHAMP
  Fashion Institute of Technology, New York

JACALYN E. S. BENNETT +
  Fashion Institute of Technology, New York

STEVEN R. BERRARD +
  Broward Community College, Florida

MICHAEL BERRY +
  Henry Ford Community College, Michigan

JEFFREY R. BRASHARES +
  University of Akron—Community and Technical College, Ohio

WILLIAM J. BRESNAN +
  South Central Technical College, Minnesota

GARY BROOKINS *
  Gulf Coast Community College, Florida

KENNETH BUNTING
  Lee College, Texas

M. ANTHONY BURNS *
  Dixie State College of Utah, Utah

CHRISTOPHER BYRON
  Norwalk Community College, Connecticut

HERB CAEN
  Sacramento City College, California

JAMES A. CARRIGG +
  Broome Community College, New York

LORRAINE CARTER +
  Edmonds Community College, Washington

HAROLD O. CHITWOOD +
  Snead State Community College, Alabama

DAVID CHU
  Fashion Institute of Technology, New York

KENTON CLARK +
  Norwalk Community College, Connecticut

VIRGINIA G. CLARK +
  Central Carolina Technical College, South Carolina

CHARLES COLLINGWOOD
  Deep Springs College, Nevada

MARGARITA COLMENARES +
  Sacramento City College, California

WILLIAM C. CRAMER +
  St. Petersburg Junior College, Florida

CURTIS J. CRAWFORD +
  Joliet Junior College, Illinois

JOY HERFEL CRONIN
  Fashion Institute of Technology, New York

JERRY DON CRUTCHFIELD +
  Paducah Community College, Kentucky

RUBEN CRUZ +
  Fashion Institute of Technology, New York

EMORY CUNNINGHAM
  Mississippi Gulf Coast Community College, Mississippi

DENNIS CURRY
  Central Florida Community College, Florida

PETER Q. DAVIS +
  San Diego City College, California

CLARK DeLEON
  Montgomery County Community College, Pennsylvania

BENNYE DICKERSON
  Dallas County Community College District, Texas

HELEN KRAUSE DONOHUE +
  Fashion Institute of Technology, New York

THOMAS DONOVAN
  City Colleges of Chicago, Illinois

TINA P. DOUGLAS *
  Alamance Community College, North Carolina

EDWARD DuCOIN +
  Camden County College, New Jersey

MICHAEL DUFF
  Delaware County Community College, Pennsylvania

MARK WAYNE DUNDEE +
  Glendale Community College, California

EDWARD E. DURYEA +
  Technical College of the Lowcountry, South Carolina

PATRICIA S. EDELKIND +
  Southeastern Community College, North Carolina

TIMOTHY L. ELDERS +
  Illinois Central College, Illinois

MAURICE DYESS EWING +
  Central Piedmont Community College, North Carolina

RUSS EWING +
  Kennedy-King College, Illinois

BRUCE P. FaBRIZIO *
  Mt. San Antonio Community College, California

ANDREW FEZZA
  Fashion Institute of Technology, New York

WILLIAM G. FRANCIS +
Prestonsburg Community College, Kentucky

CONNIE FRANCIS-CIOFFI
Fashion Institute of Technology, New York

DENNIS FRANZ
Wilbur Wright College, Illinois

THOMAS M. FRICANO +
Erie Community College, New York

DANIEL J. FULLER +
Gateway Community College, Connecticut

LINDA GALLEN +
Manatee Community College, Florida

GIANNELLA GARRETT +
Howard Community College, Maryland

LINDA GAUNT
Fashion Institute of Technology, New York

ANN GERBER
Wilbur Wright College, Illinois

DENISE GESS
Camden County College, New Jersey

JOHN PAUL GOEBEL
Fashion Institute of Technology, New York

B. THOMAS GOLISANO +
SUNY College of Technology—Alfred, New York

GERALD H. GORDON +
Cuyahoga Community College District, Ohio

LEISTER F. GRAFFIS +
North Dakota State College of Science, North Dakota

STEDMAN GRAHAM
Weatherford College, Texas

GASBY GREELEY *
Wayne County Community College, Michigan

MARGARET GATSBY GREELEY +
Wayne County Community College, Michigan

DAVID GREENWELL +
Oklahoma City Community College, Oklahoma

JUAN GUERRA
Central Florida Community College, Florida

CAROL GUZY *
Northampton Community College, Pennsylvania

WILLIAM F. HADDAD *
St. Petersburg Junior College, Florida

HERBERT HAFIF *
Chaffey Community College, California

BILL HAIRE
Fashion Institute of Technology, New York

NORMA HARRIS +
Sierra College, California

HENRY F. HENDERSON JR. +
SUNY College of Technology—Alfred, New York

FREDERICK W. HOFFMAN +
Henry Ford Community College, Michigan

STEVEN A. HOLLAND +
Cleveland State Community College, Tennessee

MICHAEL C. HUBBARD +
Tompkins-Cortland Community College, New York

PAT HILL HUBBARD +
West Valley College, California

R. D. HUBBARD *
Butler County Community College, Kansas

JIM HUBER
Central Florida Community College, Florida

VERA CHAN ING +
North Seattle Community College, Washington

DENNIS P. JANSSEN +
Northwest Iowa Community College, Iowa

MICHAEL O. JOHNSON +
Jackson Community College, Michigan

CURT JONES +
Shawnee Community College, Illinois

ROBERTS T. JONES +
Santa Barbara City College, California

ANDREA JOVINE
Fashion Institute of Technology, New York

NORMA KAMALI
Fashion Institute of Technology, New York

KAREN KANE *
Fashion Institute of Design and Merchandising, California

RICH KARLGAARD *
Bismarck State College, North Dakota

JOHN KARNATZ +
Waubonsee Community College, Illinois

ALAN KEHLET
Joliet Junior College, Illinois

DENNIS R. KELLER +
Columbus State Community College, Ohio

CALVIN KLEIN
Fashion Institute of Technology, New York

GINA KLEIN +
Berkeley College, New Jersey

JYL KLEIN
Fashion Institute of Design and Merchandising, California

HARRY M. KROGH
McCook Junior College (now Mid-Plains Community College), Nebraska

BILL KURTIS +
Independence Community College, Kansas

ANASTASIOS KYRIAKIDES
Miami-Dade Community College, Florida

DANIEL D. LACEY +
Luzerne County Community College, Pennsylvania

KENNETH P. LACORTE +
Hudson Valley Community College, New York

JIM LEHRER *
Victoria College, Texas

RICHARD N. LEIBY +
Harrisburg Area Community College, Pennsylvania

JACK LISTANOWSKY
Fashion Institute of Technology, New York

ROBERT LOCE +
Monroe Community College, New York

ANDREW T. LOCK +
Kankakee Community College, Illinois

BARRY K. LONG +
Wake Technical Community College, North Carolina

EDWARD G. LOPEZ +
New Mexico State University—Dona Ana, New Mexico

THOMAS J. MALONE +
Pearl River Community College, Mississippi

MICHAEL MANGAN
Central Florida Community College, Florida

NANCY MARINO +
Fashion Institute of Technology, New York

DOUG MARLETTE *
Seminole Community College, Florida

ROBERT J. MARMORATO +
Alamance Community College, North Carolina

SARAH McCLENDON *
Tyler Junior College, Texas

LAWRENCE McFADDEN
Asheville-Buncombe Technical Community College, North Carolina

R. MICHAEL McKINNEY +
Rappahannock Community College, Virginia

BUSINESS, INDUSTRY, AND MEDIA
continued

AMOS R. MCMULLIAN +
Chipola Junior College, Florida

M. J. MENGE +
Pensacola Junior College, Florida

RITA I. MEYER +
Central Arizona College, Arizona

ROBERT M. MILL +
*Community College of Allegheny County,
Pennsylvania*

LUCY MORGAN +
*Pasco-Hernando Community College,
Florida*

DAVIS K. MORTENSEN +
*Mississippi Gulf Coast Community
College, Mississippi*

EDWIN R. MUENZNER +
*Three Rivers Community College,
Connecticut*

BARBARA MULLINS
*Fashion Institute of Technology,
New York*

ANNE E. NELSON +
Community College of Vermont, Vermont

JULIANA I. NIXON +
Richland Community College, Illinois

JACK R. OVERACRE JR. +
*Alamance Community College,
North Carolina*

MARTI GALOVIC PALMER
*Fashion Institute of Technology,
New York*

H. ROSS PEROT *
Texarkana College, Texas

KEITH PHILPOTT +
Pratt Community College, Kansas

JAMES E. PILMER +
Waubonsee Community College, Illinois

JANE H. PINZAUTI
*Fashion Institute of Technology,
New York*

MARJORIE H. PRIES +
Truman College, Illinois

JOAN M. QUIGLEY +
*Hudson County Community College,
New Jersey*

JOHN RADECK
*Spartanburg Methodist College,
South Carolina*

LOUIS RESNICK +
*SUNY College of Technology—Delhi,
New York*

MARY ANN RESTIVO *
*Fashion Institute of Technology,
New York*

CRAIG L. RICE +
*Minneapolis Community and Technical
College, Minnesota*

JAMES T. RIZZUTO +
Otero Junior College, Colorado

ELTON RULE
Sacramento City College, California

MELVIN SALVESON
Long Beach City College, California

CHARLES B. SCARBOROUGH III +
*Mississippi Gulf Coast Community
College, Mississippi*

JOHN M. SCHILLING +
Highland Community College, Kansas

MICHAEL SCHLOW +
*Atlantic Cape Community College,
New Jersey*

DEBBIE L. SCHWAB +
Ivy Tech State College, Indiana

RACHEL R. SELISKER +
*Wake Technical Community College,
North Carolina*

RICK SELLERS +
*Columbus State Community College,
Ohio*

MARK SENTI +
*Chippewa Valley Technical College,
Wisconsin*

DAVID N. SHAFFER +
*Northampton Community College,
Pennsylvania*

JOHN F. SHEEHAN +
Pratt Community College, Kansas

LLOYD SHOPPA +
Wharton County Junior College, Texas

JOSEPH C. SIMMONS +
Dixie State College of Utah, Utah

DELFORD M. SMITH *
Centralia College, Washington

RICHARD K. SMITH +
*Southeastern Community College,
North Carolina*

CHRISTI HARRIS SPEER
Wade College, Texas

MARY ANN STILES +
*Hillsborough Community College,
Florida*

BRAD STRINGFELLOW +
*Bessemer State Technical College,
Alabama*

RICK SWARTZWELDER +
*Lake-Sumter Community College,
Florida*

HOMER E. TAYLOR +
*West Virginia University Institute
of Technology, West Virginia*

WICK TEMPLE +
Texarkana College, Texas

JAMES J. THOME +
Pratt Community College, Kansas

MARTY THOMPSON
Lower Columbia College, Washington

DENNIS R. TOFFOLO +
*St. Clair County Community College,
Michigan*

FRANK J. URTASUN +
Southwestern College, California

TROY VALDEZ +
Pikes Peak Community College, Colorado

DAVID VILLANUEVA *
*State Center Community College
District, California*

FRANKLIN F. WALKER +
Highland Community College, Illinois

THOMAS W. WATHEN +
Vincennes University, Indiana

JAMES L. WATTS +
Columbia Basin College, Washington

ALLEN R. WEISS +
Valencia Community College, Florida

ANDREA D. WHITE +
Montgomery College, Maryland

BERTA L. WHITE +
*Meridian Community College,
Mississippi*

BOB M. WHITE +
*Cowley County Community College,
Kansas*

JOHN WHITE *
*Central Piedmont Community College,
North Carolina*

BRUCE S. WILKINSON +
Delgado Community College, Louisiana

JAMES H. WILLIAMS +
*Central Florida Community College,
Florida*

STANDISH E. WILLIS +
Malcolm X College, Illinois

MICHAEL WILSON +
Highland Community College, Kansas

ZIG ZIGLAR
Hinds Community College, Mississippi

KEVIN ZRALY
*Ulster County Community College,
New York*

EDUCATION, LITERATURE, AND ARTS

MARTIN AIMES
*Dallas County Community College
District, Texas*

ALLAN C. ANDERSON +
Miles Community College, Montana

GEORGE A. BAKER III
*Warren Wilson Junior College
(now Warren Wilson College, four-year),
North Carolina*

DAVID M. BARTLEY +
*Holyoke Community College,
Massachusetts*

ELEANOR TAYLOR BLAND +
College of Lake County, Illinois

YVONNE GALLEGOS BODLE +
Ventura College, California

REX BRANDT
*Riverside Community College,
California*

GWENDOLYN BROOKS *
Kennedy-King College, Illinois

RITA MAE BROWN *
Broward Community College, Florida

OCTAVIA BUTLER
Pasadena City College, California

LANCE CARLSON +
Rio Hondo College, California

BEN W. CARR JR. +
Southeast Community College, Kentucky

KIT CARSON
Yavapai College, Arizona

DORIS LEADER CHARGE *
Salish Kootenai College, Montana

RACHEL CHEN
*Collin County Community College
District, Texas*

GRACE CLARK +
Tidewater Community College, Virginia

MAX ALLAN COLLINS JR. +
Muscatine Community College, Iowa

BRIAN CONLEY +
Sacramento City College, California

PAT COOK
Lon Morris College, Texas

RICARDO CORTEZ CRUZ +
Richland Community College, Illinois

COPELAND DAVIS
Seminole Community College, Florida

BILLY DEAN +
*East Central Community College,
Mississippi*

ELDON DENINI
Hartnell College, California

CHERYL ELIZABETH DOETCH +
*Truckee Meadows Community College,
Nevada*

DAVID HERBERT DONALD +
Holmes Community College, Mississippi

DANIEL DREISBACH +
*Greenville Technical College,
South Carolina*

WILLIAM "BILL" DUKE *
Dutchess Community College, New York

KATHERINE DUNHAM
Joliet Junior College, Illinois

MAUREEN DUNNE +
College of DuPage, Illinois

N. DEAN ECKHOFF +
Pratt Community College, Kansas

GLEN EDEN
DeKalb Technical Institute, Georgia

CAROLE FINLEY EDMONDS +
Kellogg Community College, Michigan

KAT EPPLE
Edison Community College, Florida

GERALDINE A. EVANS +
*Rochester Community and Technical
College, Minnesota*

MICHAEL FARMER +
*Greenville Technical College, South
Carolina*

JOE FRANTZ
Weatherford College, Texas

FRED FRIENDLY
*Nichols Junior College (now Nichols
College, four-year), Massachusetts*

JOHN K. GAMMAN +
Feather River College, California

HENRY LOUIS GATES JR. +
Potomac State College, West Virginia

DAVID A. GRANT +
Orange Coast College, California

LLOYD V. HACKLEY +
*Northwestern Michigan College,
Michigan*

JOHN HANNAH *
*Grand Rapids Community College,
Michigan*

EVELYN HARDY +
Broward Community College, Florida

MARILYN HARRIS
Cottey College, Missouri

L. C. HOPES +
*Gateway Community College,
Connecticut*

GREGG HUBBARD
Seminole Community College, Florida

PATRICIA M. HURLEY +
County College of Morris, New Jersey

FINIS JEFFERS
Hartnell College, California

CHRISTINE JOHNSON +
Fresno City College, California

SANDRA HILTON JOHNSTON +
*Brunswick Community College,
North Carolina*

RON JONES +
Clackamas Community College, Oregon

IDA JULIAN +
*Bucks County Community College,
Pennsylvania*

JULIA A. KEEHNER +
Highland Community College, Illinois

GREGORY KONDOS
Sacramento City College, California

JOSEPH LANGLAND
Santa Ana College, California

JOHN LANKFORD
Vincennes University, Indiana

ROBERT LAWLESS +
Lee College, Texas

ADELE LESSMEISTER +
College of DuPage, Illinois

BELLA LEWITZKY +
*San Bernardino Valley College,
California*

RICHARD LOCKRIDGE
*The Metropolitan Community Colleges,
Missouri*

JOSEPH A. MALIK +
Grays Harbor College, Washington

RAY MARSHALL *
Hinds Community College, Mississippi

CHEROKEE PAUL McDONALD
Broward Community College, Florida

RICHARD W. MIKSAD +
*Westchester Community College,
New York*

JOSEPH P. MODICA +
Trinidad State Junior College, Colorado

STEPHEN MONTAGUE
St. Petersburg Junior College, Florida

DANIEL NAKAMURA *
Rio Hondo College, California

JUDY F. NWACHIE +
Austin Community College, Texas

LOUIS D. OWENS +
Cuesta College, California

EDUARDO J. PADRON +
*Miami-Dade Community College,
Florida*

AMERICO PEREZ
*University of Texas at Brownsville
and Texas Southmost College, Texas*

OUIDA PETERSON +
Mountain View College, Texas

LANE PHALEN +
*Illinois Valley Community College,
Illinois*

THOMAS PHILLIPS
Hinds Community College, Mississippi

DAVID R. PIERCE *
Fullerton College, California

CALEB PIRTIE
Kilgore College, Texas

JAMES R. PRUCNAL +
*Gadsden State Community College,
Alabama*

RITA SIMS QUILLEN
*Mountain Empire Community College,
Virginia*

CLIFFORD E. RAY +
*Bessemer State Technical College,
Alabama*

ROD RISLEY *
San Jacinto College, Texas

CRAIG A. ROGERS +
Vermont Technical College, Vermont

JOHN E. ROUECHE +
*Mitchell Community College,
North Carolina*

MARY A. SELAK +
Trinidad State Junior College, Colorado

MARILYN L. SETINA +
Richland Community College, Illinois

SAM SHEPARD
*Mt. San Antonio Community College,
California*

LYNNE SHUSTER +
*Niagara County Community College,
New York*

LAWRENCE J. SIMPSON +
*Cuyahoga Community College District,
Ohio*

BYRON SKINNER
City Colleges of Chicago, Illinois

PATRICK D. SMITH
Hinds Community College, Mississippi

RAYMOND W. SMOCK +
South Suburban College, Illinois

EDGAR SNOW
*The Metropolitan Community Colleges,
Missouri*

GEORGE T. STANLEY +
*Southwestern Community College,
North Carolina*

CAROL M. SWAIN +
*Virginia Western Community College,
Virginia*

GLADYS SWARTHOUT
*The Metropolitan Community Colleges,
Missouri*

THOMAS J. SWITZER +
*Marshalltown Community College (now
Iowa Valley Community College
District), Iowa*

CLIFTON L. TAULBERT +
Tulsa Community College, Oklahoma

DONALD TERRAS +
Oakton Community College, Illinois

VIRGIL THOMSON
*The Metropolitan Community Colleges,
Missouri*

WAYNE D. WATSON +
Joliet Junior College, Illinois

NOFFLET D. WILLIAMS +
*Southern Union State Community
College, Alabama*

JOHN W. WRIGHT II +
*South Florida Community College,
Florida*

KENNETH YGLESIAS +
St. Petersburg Junior College, Florida

CHARLES E. YOUNG +
*San Bernardino Valley College,
California*

DAN YOUNG
*East Central Community College,
Mississippi*

ENTERTAINMENT

DUANE ALLEN
Paris Junior College, Texas

VALERIO AZZOLI +
Seneca College, Canada

CARROLL BAKER
St. Petersburg Junior College, Florida

JAMES BELUSHI *
College of DuPage, Illinois

ANNETTE BENING
San Diego Mesa College, California

JERRY CLOWER +
*Southwest Mississippi Community
College, Mississippi*

LYNNETTE COLE
*Columbia State Community College,
Tennessee*

JEFF COOK +
*Gadsden State Community College,
Alabama*

BILLY CRYSTAL +
Nassau Community College, New York

JANE CURTIN
*Elizabeth Seton Junior College, New
York*

CLIVE CUSSLER
Orange Coast College, California

PAM DAWBER
Oakland Community College, Michigan

HOWIE DOROUGH
Valencia Community College, Florida

SANDY DUNCAN
Lon Morris College, Texas

CHARLES S. DUTTON *
*Hagerstown Community College,
Maryland*

CLINT EASTWOOD
Los Angeles City College, California

DENNIS FARINO
City Colleges of Chicago, Illinois

CHRIS FONSECA +
Trinidad State Junior College, Colorado

MORGAN FREEMAN
Los Angeles City College, California

JOHN FUSCO
*Naugatuck Valley Community College,
Connecticut*

BOYD GAINES +
Allan Hancock College, California

RUDY GATLIN
Odessa College, Texas

LOU GRAMM +
Monroe Community College, New York

KIM M. GREENE *
*Central Piedmont Community College,
North Carolina*

SHARON GREYTAK +
*Housatonic Community College,
Connecticut*

TOM HANKS
Chabot College, California

WILLIAM HANNA
*Compton Community College,
California*

VY HIGGINSEN *
*Fashion Institute of Technology,
New York*

FAITH HILL
Hinds Community College, Mississippi

DUSTIN HOFFMAN
Santa Monica College, California

WILLIAM HOLDEN
Pasadena City College, California

JAN HOOKS
Edison Community College, Florida

DAVID JENKINS
Seminole Community College, Florida

DIANE KEATON
Orange Coast College, California

KATIE KELLEY +
*Santa Fe Community College,
New Mexico*

BEN KINCLOW
Southwest Texas Junior College, Texas

CHRIS KIRKPATRICK
Valencia Community College, Florida

CALVIN LEVELS
*Cuyahoga Community College District,
Ohio*

JOAN LUNDEN
American River College, California

MARK MANCINA *
Golden West College, California

MONTE MARKHAM +
Palm Beach Community College, Florida

JEFF McCARTHY +
Allan Hancock College, California

DEBORAH E. McDONALD +
Southwest Missouri State University—
West Plains, Missouri

REGINALD McKNIGHT *
Pikes Peak Community College, Colorado

JOHN MELLENCAMP
Vincennes University, Indiana

NATALIE MERCHANT
Jamestown Community College,
New York

LEE MERIWETHER *
City College of San Francisco, California

JON NAKAMATSU *
Foothill College, California

CHUCK NEGRON
Allan Hancock College, California

NICK NOLTE +
Phoenix College, Arizona

RANDY OWEN *
Northeast Alabama Community College,
Alabama

ROSIE PEREZ
Los Angeles City College, California

BILL PULLMAN
SUNY College of Technology—Delhi,
New York

QUEEN LATIFAH
Borough of Manhattan Community
College, New York

KATHARINE ROSS
Santa Rosa Junior College, California

MARTHA SCOTT
The Metropolitan Community Colleges,
Missouri

WARREN SKAAREN
Rochester Community and Technical
College, Minnesota

SHAWNTEL SMITH *
Westark College, Arkansas

STEPHEN SPINELLA +
Phoenix College, Arizona

SYLVESTER STALLONE
Miami-Dade Community College,
Florida

BOBBY THIGPEN
Seminole Community College, Florida

PHIL TIPPETT
Palomar College, California

DANIEL THOMAS TRUMAN +
Dixie State College of Utah, Utah

TOMMY TUNE
Lon Morris College, Texas

JOHN E. WALSH *
Cayuga County Community College,
New York

WAYNE WANG
Foothill College, California

ROBIN WILLIAMS
College of Marin, California

MARY BADHAM WILT
J. Sargeant Reynolds Community
College, Virginia

LEE ANN WOMACK
South Plains College, Texas

JOHN J. WOOTEN +
Camden County College, New Jersey

HEALTH, MEDICINE, AND SCIENCE

DANIEL G. AMEN +
Orange Coast College, California

JUAN ARRIAGA +
North Lake College, Texas

ELIZABETH ASHBROOK +
Patrick Henry Community College,
Virginia

STEVE BALLARD +
Southwest Tennessee Community
College, Tennessee

CLARENCE J. BECK +
Pratt Community College, Kansas

WILLIAM F. BENEDICT +
Orange County Community College,
New York

STEFAN A. BLEDIG
Southeastern Illinois College, Illinois

ARTHUR D. BOYT +
Crowder College, Missouri

MICHAEL T. CAUGHEY +
Tidewater Community College, Virginia

DONALD CHU
Ohlone College, California

FRANCIS CHUCKER +
Itasca Community College, Minnesota

CHAD CRAVATTA +
Richland Community College, Illinois

EUGENE DONG +
Hartnell College, California

PRISCILLA DOWLEN +
Lee College, Texas

SYLVIA EARLE
St. Petersburg Junior College, Florida

DOUGLAS FIELDS +
De Anza College, California

JIM FLUCKEY +
Clovis Community College, New Mexico

KATHLEEN FOX-TENNANT +
West Virginia Northern Community
College, West Virginia

REATHEL GEARY
Asheville-Buncombe Technical
Community College, North Carolina

JAMES T. GOODRICH +
Orange Coast College, California

K. KRISTENE KOONTZ GUGLIUZZA *
Lake Land College, Illinois

BLAIR W. GUSTAFSON +
Sheridan College, Wyoming

VAL J. HALAMANDARIS +
College of Eastern Utah, Utah

JAN HAUN +
Johnson County Community College,
Kansas

DANIEL HAYES
Spartanburg Methodist College, South
Carolina

CYNTHIA T. HENDERSON *
Malcolm X College, Illinois

LaVERNE H. HESS +
Chaffey Community College, California

KENNETH HUFFMAN
North Platte Junior College (now Mid-
Plains Community College), Nebraska

MARTY HURLEY +
Southern West Virginia Community
and Technical College, West Virginia

MICHAEL HUTCHINS +
Highline Community College,
Washington

LEE A. HUTTON +
Galveston College, Texas

BARBARA GIFT JACOBELLI +
Alamance Community College,
North Carolina

BETH KALNINS
Highland Community College, Kansas

JOE BEN LaGRONE +
Panola College, Texas

RENEE B. LEDFORD +
Lenoir Community College,
North Carolina

LOUIS LEO
Ulster County Community College,
New York

JACQUES P. LEVEILLE +
Bristol Community College,
Massachusetts

HENRY L. LEWIS
East Central Community College,
Mississippi

JANICE MELINDA LIVENGOOD +
Columbia State Community College,
Tennessee

MICHAEL J. MacDONALD +
Brevard Community College, Florida

STEPHEN H. MacDONALD +
Brevard Community College, Florida

HEALTH, MEDICINE, AND SCIENCE
continued

RICHARD G. MAJORS III +
Cayuga County Community College, New York

JOSEPH MANNO +
Bergen Community College, New Jersey

ANN H. MANTEL +
Jefferson Davis Community College, Alabama

MARY LOU MARZIAN +
Jefferson Community College, Kentucky

JAMES G. MCCLELLAND +
College of Lake County, Illinois

KAREN KAY MEDVILLE *
Pikes Peak Community College, Colorado

MARGARET MERKEL +
Cumberland County College, New Jersey

ROGER MITTLEMAN +
Miami-Dade Community College, Florida

SUSAN MOORE +
Truman College, Illinois

EBBIE MURRAY +
Alamance Community College, North Carolina

STEPHEN W. NICHOLAS +
Casper College, Wyoming

MALINDA BYRD NIX +
Chattahoochee Valley Community College, Alabama

BEVERLY HENRY OLIPHANT
East Central Community College, Mississippi

ELAINE A. OSTRANDER +
Yakima Valley Community College, Washington

JANUS LONG PEMBERTON +
Roane State Community College, Tennessee

JOHN M. PEZZUTO +
Atlantic Cape Community College, New Jersey

MARK A. PIERCE +
John A. Logan College, Illinois

LENARD L. POLITTE +
Mineral Area College, Missouri

WILLIAM L. ROPER +
Florida College, Florida

CUAUHTEMOC SANCHEZ
College of Oceaneering, California

NANCY SCHRYER +
Waukesha County Technical College, Wisconsin

RICHARD M. SCRUSHY *
Jefferson State Community College, Alabama

MARCELINA J. T. SMITH +
Cape Cod Community College, Massachusetts

ROBERT F. SPETZLER *
Illinois Valley Community College, Illinois

MARIE M. SPIVEY +
Capital Community College— Woodland, Connecticut

LINDA E. STONE +
Union County College, New Jersey

BEVERLY A. SZUKIS +
Jefferson Community College, Kentucky

J. CRAIG VENTER *
College of San Mateo, California

RUTH WALTON +
Bunker Hill Community College, Massachusetts

LAMAR WEEMS
East Central Community College, Mississippi

VICKI WEISMAN +
El Centro College, Texas

ELIZABETH A. WETZEL *
Richland Community College, Illinois

RICHARD W. ZAHN +
Allen County Community College, Kansas

MICHAEL F. ZANAKIS +
Indian River Community College, Florida

MILITARY AND SPACE

MILDRED "MICKY" TUTTLE AXTON *
Coffeyville Community College, Kansas

WILLIAM R. BARRETT
Southeastern Illinois College, Illinois

ERIC W. BENKEN +
Community College of the Air Force, Alabama

WILLIAM F. BUNDY +
Leeward Community College, Hawaii

CLIFFORD E. CHARLESWORTH
Hinds Community College, Mississippi

EILEEN M. COLLINS *
Corning Community College, New York

FRANCIS D. DEMASI +
Luzerne County Community College, Pennsylvania

SAMUEL T. DURRANCE +
St. Petersburg Junior College, Florida

ROBERT FRIETAG
Jackson Community College, Michigan

ROBERT L. "HOOT" GIBSON *
Suffolk County Community College, New York

FRED A. GORDEN *
Kellogg Community College, Michigan

KEITH GORDON
Spartanburg Methodist College, South Carolina

FRED W. HAISE *
Mississippi Gulf Coast Community College, Mississippi

BEN D. HANCOCK +
Central Arizona College, Arizona

DARYL R. HANCOCK +
John A. Logan College, Illinois

MELISSA BROWN HERKT +
Gadsden State Community College, Alabama

B. R. "BOBBY" INMAN
Tyler Junior College, Texas

SAMUEL O. MASSEY *
Holmes Community College, Mississippi

JAMES A. MCDIVITT *
Jackson Community College, Michigan

WILLIAM POTTS
Rogers University, Oklahoma

FRANCIS R. SCOBEE +
San Antonio College, Texas

EDWARD C. STONE +
Southeastern Community College, Iowa

DAVID OGDEN "BUD" THOMS +
Jones County Junior College, Mississippi

TERRY W. TILTON +
Kirkwood Community College, Iowa

DOUGLAS C. VERISSIMO *
Cape Cod Community College, Massachusetts

RICHARD WELCH
Berkshire Community College, Massachusetts

PUBLIC SERVICE, GOVERNMENT, AND NONPROFIT

FOSTER ANDERSEN
Monroe Community College, New York

BILL ANOATUBBY *
Murray State College, Oklahoma

J. KEITH ARNOLD +
Edison Community College, Florida

MIKE BALD +
Highland Community College, Illinois

ROSE MARIE BATTISTI *
Herkimer County Community College, New York

JEFFREY BEAN +
Mount Wachusett Community College, Massachusetts

STEPHEN BEAN +
Richland Community College, Illinois

BETTY STANLEY BEENE
Texarkana College, Texas

K. MICHAEL BENZ +
Cuyahoga Community College District, Ohio

DOTTIE BERGER +
Hillsborough Community College, Florida

DONNA TOEPFER BINKLEY +
Highland Community College, Illinois

DON BONKER
Clark College, Washington

F. ALLEN BOYD +
North Florida Community College, Florida

JACK BROOKS +
Lamar State College—Orange, Texas

HERBERT BROWN
San Antonio College, Texas

MARTHA RIDDLE BROWN
Spartanburg Methodist College, South Carolina

CAROL M. BROWNER *
Miami-Dade Community College, Florida

BOB BULLOCK +
Hill College, Texas

ALBERT BUSTAMONTE
San Antonio College, Texas

LEONARD G. BUTLER +
Northland Pioneer College, Arizona

JAMES M. CAHILL +
Middlesex County College, New Jersey

BONNIE J. CAMPBELL +
Des Moines Area Community College, Iowa

JACK M. CAMPBELL +
Hutchinson Community College, Kansas

TAMMY S. CAMPBELL +
Richland Community College, Illinois

CHRISTINE CANAVAN +
Massasoit Community College, Massachusetts

DAVID CARGO
Jackson Community College, Michigan

ROBERTO CARMONA +
Sauk Valley Community College, Illinois

BENJAMIN J. CAYETANO *
Los Angeles Harbor College, California

KATHLEEN R. CLAY +
Western Piedmont Community College, North Carolina

EDIE CONNELLY +
North Harris Montgomery Community College District, Texas

JOSEPH A. COSTELLO JR. +
Monroe County Community College, Michigan

F. JANE COTTON
Jackson Community College, Michigan

HENRY CUELLAR +
Laredo Community College, Texas

RONALD DELLUMS
Oakland City College, Michigan

MARILYN L. DeSHIELDS +
Cape Cod Community College, Massachusetts

MICHAEL R. DRESSLER +
Bergen Community College, New Jersey

DAWNNA DUKES
Austin Community College, Texas

GEORGE R. DUNLAP +
Central Piedmont Community College, North Carolina

BRIAN J. EARLEY +
Anne Arundel Community College, Maryland

CLAUDIA L. EDWARDS
Bronx Community College, New York

MARGARITA ESQUIROZ *
Miami-Dade Community College, Florida

LANE EVANS +
Black Hawk College, Illinois

CHAKA FATTAH
Community College of Philadelphia, Pennsylvania

CHARLES S. FLEMING *
Bronx Community College, New York

ROBERT GAMMAGE
Del Mar College, Texas

REYNALDO G. GARZA *
University of Texas at Brownsville and Texas Southmost College, Texas

SAM GEJDENSON
Mitchell College, Connecticut

PARRIS N. GLENDENING *
Broward Community College, Florida

ARTHUR GOLDBERG
Crane Junior College (now Malcolm X College), Illinois

HENRY B. GONZALEZ *
San Antonio College, Texas

STEVEN GOOD +
Moraine Valley Community College, Illinois

KAREN E. GORDON +
Hudson Valley Community College, New York

THOMAS P. GORDON +
Delaware Technical and Community College, Delaware

MARY ELIZABETH "TIPPER" GORE
Garland Junior College, Massachusetts

WILLIAM GRACE +
Berkshire Community College, Massachusetts

ROD GRAMS
Anoka-Ramsey Community College, Minnesota

SUNNY-BRENT HARDING +
Fisher College, Massachusetts

CLARENCE HARMON +
St. Louis Community College, Missouri

DENIS HAYES
Clark College, Washington

SUE HECHT +
Frederick Community College, Maryland

GEORGE HIGH
Eastern A&M Junior College (now Eastern Oklahoma State College), Oklahoma

JEFFREY R. HOLLAND +
Dixie State College of Utah, Utah

PAM B. JACKMAN BROWN +
Borough of Manhattan Community College, New York

MICHAEL W. JONES +
San Jacinto College, Texas

TERRY KEEL
Austin Community College, Texas

ALLAN K. KEHL +
Gateway Technical College, Wisconsin

JOYCE LUTHER KENNARD +
Pasadena City College, California

JEANE J. KIRKPATRICK
Stephens College (now four-year), Missouri

ELSIE LACY +
Lamar Community College, Colorado

RAY LaHOOD +
Illinois Central College, Illinois

LARRY P. LANGFORD +
Lawson State Community College, Alabama

THOMAS W. LIBOUS +
Broome Community College, New York

PAMELA SUE LYCHNER +
Houston Community College System, Texas

EILEEN LYONS +
College of DuPage, Illinois

EDWARD MADIGAN
Lincoln College, Illinois

SUSAN M. MANN +
Butler County Community College, Kansas

BLANCHE MANNING
City Colleges of Chicago, Illinois

AWILDA R. MARQUEZ *
Harford Community College, Maryland

PUBLIC SERVICE, GOVERNMENT, AND NONPROFIT, *continued*

MATTHEW G. MARTINEZ
Los Angeles Trade-Technical College, California

DAVID MATHIS +
Mohawk Valley Community College, New York

STEVE MCDANIEL +
Jackson State Community College, Tennessee

W. DAVID MCFADYEN JR. +
Craven Community College, North Carolina

KWEISI MFUME *
Baltimore City Community College, Maryland

GEORGE MILLER +
Diablo Valley College, California

WILLIAM "FISH BAIT" MILLER
Mississippi Gulf Coast Community College, Mississippi

JUSTIN SMITH MORRILL +
Vermont Technical College, Vermont

RUDOLPH J. MUNIS +
Trinidad State Junior College, Colorado

RICHARD A. MURRAY +
Brookhaven College, Texas

DAVID R. "RONNIE" MUSGROVE +
Northwest Mississippi Community College, Mississippi

FRANCINE NEFF
Cottey College, Missouri

JACK O'CONNELL +
Ventura College, California

STAN OFTELIE +
Cypress College, California

BEVERLY O'NEILL +
Long Beach City College, California

ALEX H. OROZCO +
St. Augustine College, Illinois

SOLOMON P. ORTIZ
Del Mar College, Texas

KARLA M. OSANTOWSKI +
Harold Washington College, Illinois

STEPHEN C. PADILLA +
Southwestern College, California

RUDY PERPICH *
Hibbing Community College: A Technical and Community College, Minnesota

CHARLES PICKERING
East Central Community College, Mississippi

BRENDA PREMO *
Golden West College, California

ROBERT PRESLEY +
Riverside Community College, California

T. EUCLID RAINS SR. +
Snead State Community College, Alabama

ROBERTO RAMIREZ +
Bronx Community College, New York

SILVESTRE REYES
El Paso Community College District, Texas

ELVIRA REYNA +
Eastfield College, Texas

CYNTHIA RIAL-COLÓN +
University of Puerto Rico at Aguadilla, Puerto Rico

NORMAN B. RICE *
Highline Community College, Washington

HAROLD RODRIGUEZ +
Truman College, Illinois

MATT RODRIGUEZ
Wilbur Wright College, Illinois

JAMES E. ROGAN +
Las Positas Community College, California

ILEANA ROS-LEHTINEN
Miami-Dade Community College, Florida

CALVIN ROSS +
Miami-Dade Community College, Florida

RUTH RYAN
Alvin Community College, Texas

MATT SALMON +
Mesa Community College, Arizona

ANNETTE M. SANDBERG +
Big Bend Community College, Washington

GEORGE E. SANGMEISTER +
Joliet Junior College, Illinois

VINCENT C. SCHOEMEHL JR. +
St. Louis Community College, Missouri

KEVIN P. SCULLY +
Community College of Vermont, Vermont

DAVID H. SHINN *
Yakima Valley Community College, Washington

PETER SIKORA
Cuyahoga Community College District, Ohio

JOHN SISCO
Morton College, Illinois

JOSE SOSA +
Burlington County College, New Jersey

LELAND A. SPENCER +
Tri-County Community College, North Carolina

CHARLES STENHOLM
Tarleton State Junior College (now Tarleton State University), Texas

MICHAEL A. STOKKE +
Illinois Central College, Illinois

HILDA TAGLE +
Del Mar College, Texas

CHARLES E. TAYLOR +
Western Piedmont Community College, North Carolina

MAXWELL TAYLOR
The Metropolitan Community Colleges, Missouri

WILLIAM THOMAS
Santa Ana College, California

BENNIE THOMPSON
Hinds Community College, Mississippi

FLETCHER THOMPSON
Spartanburg Methodist College, South Carolina

ESTHER MOELLERING TOMLJANOVICH +
Itasca Community College, Minnesota

ESTEBAN TORRES
East Los Angeles College, California

FERNANDO M. TORRES-GIL +
Hartnell College, California

MARVENA TWIGG +
Columbus State Community College, Ohio

CARLOS VALDEZ +
Del Mar College, Texas

BECKY W. WALLACE +
Montgomery Community College, North Carolina

PORTIA L. WALLACE +
College of Lake County, Illinois

RUDY WASHINGTON +
City University of New York, New York

DIANE E. WATSON +
Los Angeles City College, California

WELLINGTON E. WEBB +
Northeastern Junior College, Colorado

WINIFRED S. WEISLOGEL +
Union County College, New Jersey

RONNIE L. WHITE +
St. Louis Community College, Missouri

LUANNE WILLS-MERRELL +
Lansing Community College, Michigan

JEROME R. WOLFF +
Waukesha County Technical College, Wisconsin

Robert C. Wrenn +
Southside Virginia Community College, Virginia

Jim Wright +
Weatherford College, Texas

Don Young
Yuba College, California

SPORTS

Rich Amaral
Orange Coast College, California

Kevin Appier +
Antelope Valley College, California

Richie Ashburn
Norfolk Junior College (now Northeast Community College), Virginia

David Benoit
Tyler Junior College, Texas

Ote Berry
Eastern Wyoming College, Wyoming

Buddy Black
Lower Columbia College, Washington

Isaac Bruce
Santa Monica College, California

Van Chancellor +
East Central Community College, Mississippi

Roger Clemens
San Jacinto College, Texas

Rheal P. Cormier +
Community College of Rhode Island, Rhode Island

Danny Cox
Chattahoochee Valley Community College, Alabama

Steve Francis
Hagerstown Community College, Maryland

David Fredman +
John A. Logan College, Illinois

John Gagliardi +
Trinidad State Junior College, Colorado

Cynthia Ann Gettinger
Manatee Community College, Florida

Brad Gilbert
Foothill College, California

Lee Haney
Spartanburg Methodist College, South Carolina

Dionna M. Harris +
Delaware Technical and Community College, Delaware

John Hart
Seminole Community College, Florida

Thomas Henderson
San Jacinto College, Texas

Lionel E. Hollins +
Dixie State College of Utah, Utah

Frederick Hood
San Jose City College, California

Ewing Kauffman
Kansas City Kansas Community College

Andy Kindle +
Kaskaskia College, Illinois

Patrick Listach +
McLennan Community College, Texas

Bob McAdoo
Vincennes University, Indiana

Sam Mack
Tyler Junior College, Texas

Jerry Martin
Spartanburg Methodist College, South Carolina

Bernadette Mattox +
Roane State Community College, Tennessee

Warren Moon
West Los Angeles College, California

Nat Moore
Miami-Dade Community College, Florida

Jaime Navarro *
Miami-Dade Community College, Florida

Robert Pack
Tyler Junior College, Texas

Tom Pagnozzi +
Central Arizona College, Arizona

Mikael Pernfors
Seminole Community College, Florida

Bridget Pettis +
Central Arizona College, Arizona

Kirby Puckett
Triton College, Illinois

Thomas P. "Pete" Rademacher +
Yakima Valley Community College, Washington

Gary Redus +
Calhoun Community College, Alabama

Mitch Richmond
Moberly Area Community College, Missouri

Jackie Robinson
Pasadena City College, California

Alvin "Pete" Rozelle
Compton Community College, California

Nolan Ryan +
Alvin Community College, Texas

Reggie Sanders
Spartanburg Methodist College, South Carolina

Kevin V. Saunders *
Del Mar College, Texas

Bob Seagren
Mt. San Antonio Community College, California

Dwight Smith
Spartanburg Methodist College, South Carolina

Don Sutton *
Gulf Coast Community College, Florida

Rick Sweet
Lower Columbia College, Washington

Sheryl Swoopes
South Plains College, Texas

Cathy Turner +
Monroe Community College, New York

Dick Vermeil
Napa Valley College, California

Bill Walsh
College of San Mateo, California

Anthony "Spud" Webb
Midland College, Texas

Archie Williams
College of San Mateo, California

Venus Williams
Palm Beach Community College, Florida

William "Mookie" Wilson
Spartanburg Methodist College, South Carolina

Frank "Fuzzy" Zoeller
Edison Community College, Florida

Past AACC Board Chairs

1920 JAMES M. WOOD
Stephens College, Missouri

1921 DAVID MACKENZIE
Detroit Junior College, Michigan

1922 GEORGE WINFIELD
Whitworth College, Mississippi

1923 JAMES M. WOOD
Stephens College, Missouri

1924 JAMES M. WOOD
Stephens College, Missouri

1925 L. E. PLUMMER
Fullerton Junior College, California

1926 H. E. NOFFSINGER
Virginia Intermont College, Virginia

1927 L. W. SMITH
Joliet Junior College, Illinois

1928 EDGAR D. LEE
Christian College, Missouri

1929 J. THOMAS DAVIS
John Tarleton College, Texas

1930 JOHN BARTON
Ward-Belmont School, Tennessee

1931 JEREMIAH LILLIARD
*Sacramento Junior College,
California*

1932 RICHARD G. COX
Gulf Park College, Mississippi

1933 ARTHUR I. ANDREWS
*Grand Rapids Junior College,
Michigan*

1934 A. M. HITCH
Kemper Military School, Missouri

1935 E. Q. BROTHERS
Little Rock Junior College, Arkansas

1936 ROBERT TREVORROW
Centenary Junior College, New Jersey

1937 W. W. HAGGARD
Joliet Junior College, Illinois

1938 KATHERINE DENWORTH
*Bradford Junior College,
Massachusetts*

1939 NICHOLAS RICCIARDI
*San Bernardino Junior College,
California*

1940 BYRON HOLLINSHEAD
*Scranton-Keystone Junior College,
Pennsylvania*

1941 C. C. COLVERT
Northeast Junior College, Louisiana

1942 J. C. MILLER
Christian College, Missouri

1943 JOHN W. HARBESON
Pasadena Junior College, California

1944 JESSE P. BOGUE
*Green Mountain Junior College,
Vermont*

1945 ROY W. GODDARD
Rochester Junior College, Minnesota

1946 LAWRENCE L. BETHEL
*New Haven YMCA Junior College,
Connecticut*

1947 R. C. INGALLS
*East Los Angeles Junior College,
California*

1948 EUGENE FARLEY
*Bucknell University and Junior
College, Pennsylvania*

1949 L. L. MEDSKER
*Wright Branch Chicago Junior
College, Illinois*

1950 CURTIS BISHOP
Averett College, Virginia

1951 EUGENE B. CHAFFEE
Boise Junior College, Idaho

1952 DOROTHY BELL
*Bradford Junior College,
Massachusetts*

1953 BASIL PETERSON
Orange Coast College, California

1954 FREDERICK MARSTON
Kemper Military School, Missouri

1955 HUGH PRICE
*Montgomery Junior College,
Maryland*

1956 EDWARD SCHLAEFFER
*Monmouth Junior College,
New Jersey*

1957 JAMES EWING
*Copiah-Lincoln Junior College,
Mississippi*

1958 EDMUND J. GLEAZER JR.
Graceland College, Iowa

1959 GEORGE KIDLOW
North Idaho Junior College, Idaho

1960 MARVIN KNUDSON
Pueblo Junior College, Colorado

1961 HENRY LITTLEFIELD
*Junior College of University of
Bridgeport, Connecticut*

1962 OSCAR EDINGER JR.
*Mt. San Antonio Junior College,
California*

1963 CHARLES HARMAN
Bluefield College, Virginia

1964 DONALD DEYO
*Montgomery Junior College,
Maryland*

1965 KENNETH FREEMAN
Christian College, Missouri

1966 DWIGHT BAIRD
Clark College, Washington

1967 BILL J. PRIEST
*Dallas County Community College
District, Texas*

1968 DONALD ELDRIDGE
Bennett College, New York

1969 STUART MARSEE
El Camino College, California

1970 EVERETT WOODMAN
*Colby Junior College, New
Hampshire*

1971 CHARLES CHAPMAN
Cuyahoga Community College, Ohio

1972 JOSEPH FORDYCE
*Santa Fe Community College,
Florida*

1973 EDWARD SIMONSON
Bakersfield Junior College, California

1974 PETER MASIKO
*Miami-Dade Community College,
Florida*

1975 PETER MASIKO
*Miami-Dade Community College,
Florida*

1976 ABEL SYKES
Compton College, California

1977 RICHARD HAGEMEYER
*Central Piedmont Community
College, North Carolina*

1978	**HELENA HOWE** *Mesa College, Arizona*	1994	**GEORGE R. BOGGS** *Palomar College, California*
1979	**JESS PARRISH** *Shelby State Technical College,* *Tennessee*	1995	**JACQUELYN BELCHER** *Minneapolis Community College,* *Minnesota*
1980	**NORMAN WATSON** *Coast Community College, California*	1996	**DANIEL MORIARTY** *Portland Community College, Oregon*
1981	**WILLIAM RAMSEY** *Milwaukee Area Technical College,* *Wisconsin*	1997	**WALTER BUMPHUS** *Brookhaven College, Texas*
1982	**JOHN CONNOLLY** *Dutchess Community College,* *New York*	1998	**AUGUSTINE P. GALLEGO** *San Diego Community College* *District, California*
1982	**JOE B. RUSHING** *Tarrant County Junior College, Texas*	1999	**P. ANTHONY ZEISS** *Central Piedmont Community* *College, North Carolina*
1983	**HAROLD D. MCANINCH** *College of DuPage, Illinois*	2000	**CAROLYN G. WILLIAMS** *Bronx Community College, New York*
1984	**BERNARD LUSKIN** *Orange Coast College, California*	2001	**CYNTHIA M. HEELAN** *Colorado Mountain College,* *Colorado*
1985	**JUDITH EATON** *Community College of Philadelphia,* *Pennsylvania*		
1986	**JOSHUA L. SMITH** *California Community Colleges,* *California*		
1987	**R. JAN LECROY** *Dallas County Community College* *District, Texas*		
1988	**LAWRENCE W. TYREE** *Gulf Coast Community College,* *Florida*		
1989	**DAVID H. PONITZ** *Sinclair Community College, Ohio*		
1990	**FLORA MANCUSO EDWARDS** *Middlesex County College,* *New Jersey*		
1991	**JOHN KEYSER** *Clackamas Community College,* *Oregon*		
1992	**DAVID E. DANIEL** *Midland College, Texas*		
1993	**BEVERLY SIMONE** *Madison Area Technical College,* *Wisconsin*		

Past AACC Chief Executive Officers

1920	GEORGE ZOOK (FOUNDER)
1920–1923	MARTHA MCKENZIE REID
1923–1938	DOAK S. CAMPBELL
1938–1945	WALTER CROSBY EELLS
1945–1946	WINIFRED R. LONG
1946–1958	JESSE P. BOGUE
1958–1981	EDMUND J. GLEAZER JR.
1981–1991	DALE PARNELL
1991–2000	DAVID R. PIERCE
2000–	GEORGE R. BOGGS

AACC Leadership Award Winners

1982	C. C. COLVERT B. LAMAR JOHNSON	1992	EDMUND J. GLEAZER JR.
1983	JOSEPH P. COSAND	1993	DALE PARNELL
1984	BILL J. PRIEST NORMAN E. WATSON	1994	RICHARD ALFRED GEORGE A. BAKER III TERRY O'BANION
1985	MARGARET MOSAL	1995	ARTHUR COHEN CAROLYN DESJARDINS ROBERT H. MCCABE
1986	JOHN E. ROUECHE		
1987	JAMES L. WATTENBARGER	1996	PAUL A. ELSNER ANNE E. MULDER GEORGE B. VAUGHAN
1988	S. V. MARTORANA		
1989	ERNEST L. BOYER	1997	SUANNE D. ROUECHE
1990	K. PATRICIA CROSS	1998	DONALD G. PHELPS
1991	THE HONORABLE WILHELMINA R. DELCO	2000	DALE F. CAMPBELL

ACKNOWLEDGMENTS

SOURCES CITED

AACC expresses sincere thanks to the many community college representatives and alumni who provided photographs and information for this work. The book was designed by Kathleen Mallow-Sager with photo editing by Jane Martin and editorial direction by Norma Kent and Donna Carey. Contributing writers were Janet Cave, Jean Crawford, Madeline Patton, Roseanne Scott, and Jarelle Stein. AACC reviewers included Lynn Barnett, George Boggs, Audree Chase, Arnold Kee, Sarah Lawler, and Gail Robinson. Christopher Shults, Frank Williams, and Kent Phillippe compiled the lists of colleges and distinguished alumni from AACC database records. Barbara L. Klein prepared the index and read proofs. Many thanks to community college historian Robert P. Pedersen, journalist Robert Blezard, and copyeditor Jan Stanley.

Unless noted below, the information and quotes in this book were drawn from interviews and personal communications, biographies submitted in connection with the AACC Outstanding Alumni Awards, or works copyrighted by AACC.

American Academy of Achievement. "Sylvia Earle, Ph.D.: Undersea Explorer." Interview, 27 January 1991. Internet: www.achievement.org.

Beene, Betty Stanley. Interview by America's Promise. Internet: www.americaspromise.org/interviews/beene.htm. Accessed 7 June 2000.

Brooks, Gwendolyn. Speech to faculty of Malone College, Ohio, 21 February 1994.

Chun, Janean. "To Tell the Truth." *Entrepreneur Magazine* 26 (4).

Cooper, Lois. "CCC brought 'Sun' shine to Jerry Gordon." *Sun Newspapers,* 22 May 1980.

Farhi, Paul. "Drama and Deliverance: After Escaping Baltimore's Streets Charles S. Dutton Captures Them on HBO." *The Washington Post,* C1, 12 April 2000.

Greenspan, Alan. Hearing of the Senate Banking, Housing, and Urban Affairs Committee, Semiannual Monetary Policy Report, 21 July 1998.

Hamilton, Kendra. "Her Poetry Talks about Life." *The Houston Chronicle,* 13, 19 April 1992.

Hoffman, Dustin. Santa Monica College Press Conference, 13 October 1999.

Howell, Beverly. "Brewton Residents Give Support to Earthquake Victims." Brewton (Ala.) *Standard,* 1995.

Jennings, Mary. "Fall of the Wild: More and More Animals Face Extinction Despite Efforts by Zoos, Conservationists." Louisville *Courier-Journal,* Metro Section, 6 October 1997.

Mfume, Kweisi. *No Free Ride: From the Mean Streets to the Mainstream.* New York: Ballantine Books, 1996.

"Miss America Speaks Out for Education." *Los Angeles Times,* 24 October 1995.

Nipper, Neil B. "Air Force Doctor Retires at 67, Keeps on Healing." *Air Force News,* 28 July 1998.

"Position Statement in Support of Associate Degree as Preparation for the Entry-Level Registered Nurse." National Organization for Associate Degree Nursing. Adopted 31 January 1998.

"PPCC Graduate Research Scientist at Arizona State University West." *Pikes Peak Community College Newsletter,* 1, 17 April 1995.

Robinson, Jackie, and Alfred Duckett. *I Never Had It Made.* New York: G. P. Putnam's Sons, 1972.

Suhler, Jayne Noble. "Campus Job Brokers." *Dallas Morning News,* C-1, 5 April 1999.

PICTURE CREDITS

Credits for illustrations from left to right are separated by semicolons; from top to bottom by dashes.

Cover: Marty Sohl; Ed Kosmicki, Colorado Mountain College—The Metropolitan Community Colleges, Missouri; Sandra Reyes, Collin County Community College, Texas;

AP/Wide World Photos. Copyright: Joliet Junior College, Illinois. Contents: Parkland College, Illinois. 4: Joliet Junior College, Illinois. 5: St. Philip's College, Texas. 6: Lansing Community College, Michigan; Bronx Community College, New York—College of San Mateo, California. 7: Highland Community College, Illinois. 8: Berkshire Community

College, Massachusetts. 9: Miami-Dade Community College, Florida; Haywood Community College, North Carolina—Parkland College, Illinois. 10: Southwest Tennessee Community College—Cuyahoga Community College, Ohio; Art Brackley. 11: Kelly & Massa Photography. 12: Miami-Dade Community College, Florida. 13: Mildred

Tuttle Axton. 14: College of San Mateo, California. 15: Colorado Northwestern Community College. 16: Northeast Wisconsin Technical College—The Metropolitan Community Colleges, Missouri. 17: Alpena Community College, Michigan—Orange Coast College, California. 18: Salem Community College, New Jersey; Texarkana College, Texas. 19: Community Colleges of Spokane, Washington. 20: DOER Marine; Michael Hutchins—North Carolina Community College System. 21: Tomball College, Texas—San Juan College, New Mexico. 22: City College of San Francisco—Santa Monica College, California. 22–23: Sinclair Community College, Ohio. 23: J. Craig Venter; North Lake College, Texas (background). 24: Sandra Reyes, Collin County Community College, Texas. 25: Miami-Dade Community College, Florida. 26: AP/Wide World Photos; NASA; Fred W. Haise—NASA; Berkshire Community College, Massachusetts. 27: Jackson Community College, Michigan. 28: Fashion Institute of Technology, New York (2). 29: Vy Higginsen; Christi Harris Speer; Dave Tillett; Nautica Enterprises, Inc.—Karen Kane; Mary Ann Restivo. 30: Waukesha County Technical College, Wisconsin; Houston Community College System, Texas. 31: El Centro College, Texas—Fashion Institute of Technology, New York (2). 32: El Centro College, Texas. 33: Collette Fournier, SUNY Rockland Community College, New York. 34, Hillsborough Community College, Florida; The Metropolitan Community Colleges, Missouri. 35: Cynthia T. Henderson; Highland Community College, Illinois—Ulster County Community College, New York; Tidewater Community College, Virginia; K. Kristene Koontz Gugliuzza. 36: Crafton Hills College, California. 37: Miami-Dade Community College, Florida. 38: Indian Hills Community College, Iowa—Cuauhtemoc Sanchez. 39: College of Oceaneering, California. 40: AACC archive—Berkshire Community College, Massachusetts. 41: Donald Chu. 42: Indian River Community College, Florida. 43: Monroe Community College, New York. 44: The Metropolitan Community Colleges, Missouri. 44–45: Northern Virginia Community College. 46: Fashion Institute of Technology, New York; Miami-Dade Community College, Florida. 47: Jim Lehrer; Sarah McClendon; Kenneth Bunting—Sacramento City College, California; Carol Guzy; Fox Television Stations. 48: Collette Fournier, SUNY Rockland Community College, New York; Waldorf College, Iowa. 49: Herkimer County Community College, New York. 50: The Dallas Morning News/Russell Bronson.

51: Northeast Wisconsin Technical College. 52: Cuyahoga Community College, Ohio—Haywood Community College, North Carolina; Burlington County College, New Jersey. 53: Bruce P. FaBrizio—Dennis Craig Curry. 54: Michael Duff—Herbert Hafif—Mary Ann Stiles. 55: Aims Community College, Colorado. 56: Reid Horn, Dallas; Thomas Golisano; Anne E. Nelson—Bradbury Anderson; Valerio Azzoli. 57: Richard M. Scrushy; Ross Perot Foundation—ZiLOG, Inc., California; Rich Karlgaard; Michael O. Johnson. 58: El Centro College, Texas. 59: Ulster County Community College, New York, and Kevin Zraly—James Lafayette. 60: Fred Adams; Finger Lakes Community College, New York—Kirkwood Community College, Iowa. 61: Johnson County Community College, Kansas. 62: Cossatot Technical College, Arkansas; Juan C. Guerra. 63: Catawba Valley Community College, North Carolina. 64: The University of Kentucky; Kevin V. Saunders. 65: Hinds Community College, Mississippi; Garrett Community College, Maryland—Indian River Community College, Florida. 66: Johnson County Community College, Kansas. 67: Ed Kirwan; Don Cochran (Turner and medal)—Cynthia Ann Gettinger; Dionna M. Harris; Yakima Valley Community College, Washington. 68: Office of Nolan Ryan; South Plains College, Texas—AP/Wide World Photos; Jaime Navarro; Bill Reid; AP/Wide World Photos. 69: © 2000 James Fain. 70: Jackson Citizen Patriot. All rights reserved. 71: Northcentral Technical College Alternative High School, Wisconsin. 72: Andrew Eccles; Northern Virginia Community College. 73: Kweisi Mfume; Claudia L. Edwards; Betty Stanley Beene—William Grace; Foster Andersen. 74: Leonard G. Butler; Rio Hondo College, California—Rio Salado College, Arizona. 75: Esther Moellering Tomljanovich—Peter M. Sikora. 76: Bill Anoatubby; Jeane J. Kirkpatrick; Carol Browner; Ray Marshall—AP/ Wide World Photos; Benjamin Cayetano; Hibbing Community College, Minnesota. 77: Ray LaHood; Norman B. Rice; Henry Gonzalez—Austin Community College, Texas; J. Keith Arnold. 78: U.S. Air Force (2)—Blue Angel PAO. 79: Art Brackley. 80–81: Crafton Hills College, California. 82: Susan Hereford, Portland Community College, Oregon. 82: Rock Valley College, Illinois. 83: Maricopa Community College District. 84: AP/Wide World Photos; Orange Coast College, California. 85: Miami-Dade Community College, Florida—San Diego Mesa College, California. 86: AP/Wide World Photos;

Joan Marcus—Fox Broadcasting Company; Lee Meriwether; Santa Monica College, California—College of DuPage, Illinois. 87: Valencia Community College, Florida. 88: City College of San Francisco. 89: John H. White. 90: Ohlone College, California; Miami-Dade Community College, Florida; Hartnell College, California. 91: Sandra Reyes, Collin County Community College, Texas—Yavapai College, Arizona. 92: St. Petersburg Junior College, Florida; Jon Y. Nakamatsu; Burnell Caldwell; Clackamus Community College, Oregon—Ron Keith; South Plains College, Texas. 93: Cottey College, Missouri. 94: Cuyahoga Community College, Ohio. 95: Northland Community and Technical College, Minnesota—Johnson County Community College, Kansas. 96: North Hennepin Community College, Minnesota; Orange Coast College, California. 97: Marty Sohl. 98: American Artists, Inc.; Jill Krementz; Rita Sims Quillen—John Fusco; AP/Wide World Photos; Clive Russ. 99: Hill College, Texas. 100: TransPacific Hawaii College; Phi Theta Kappa, Mississippi. 101: Phi Theta Kappa, Mississippi (2)—David R. Pierce. 102: Pima Community College, Arizona. 103: Phil Bell. 104: K. McKay-Erwin, Dallas County Community College District (background)—Norman Goldberg for Borough of Manhattan Community College—Frederick Community College, Maryland. 105: Ed Kosmicki, Colorado Mountain College.

INDEX